K I L

C000226066

A Hundred

Wayside Chapels

of Malta & Gozo

HERITAGE
BOOKS
2000

Published by Heritage Books,
a subsidiary of Midsea Books Ltd.
3a Strait Street, Valletta, Malta

Produced by
Mizzi Design and Graphic Services Ltd.
Printed at
Interprint (Malta) Ltd

First published in 1990
This edition 2000

Sketches and Cover Design by the author

ISBN 99909-93-05-X (Hardback)
ISBN 99909-93-06-8 (Paperback)

CONTENTS

PREFACE

The small churches of the Maltese Islands, which are such an essential feature of their urban and rural topography, have since at least 1866, when Achille Ferris published his now classic work *Descrizione storica delle chiese di Malta e Gozo*, excited the interest of both the casual visitor and the committed researcher. Their appeal is multifaceted. They are, in the first place, an eloquent testimony of the Latin Christian identity of the small Mediterranean archipelago and are so deeply rooted in its variegated history that no worthwhile study of the place can afford to bypass them. Popularly (albeit erroneously) known by the name of *kappelli*,[1] they often impress by their uncomplicated sculptural masses. Their architecture reflects the Maltese mason's response to the physical realities of a harsh environment that produces little building timber but a generous supply of soft, easily quarried limestone whose plastic qualities he learnt to exploit. The best among them are minor masterpieces of a grass-roots architectural expression whose simple syntax helped them harmonise with the built fabric of the town or village and with the rugged or pastoral setting of the countryside. Rarely, if ever, are they contextual misfits.

The history of the older and better known churches is often blurred by traditions and legends resulting from the pious fabrications of the seventeenth and early eighteenth centuries when the need to stress the Christian European identity of the Maltese was particularly acute.[2] Such myths sometimes have a charm that contributes to the romantic appeal of the building. They are therefore part of its heritage and as such deserve to be recalled and transmitted to posterity. Proper care should, however, be taken to distance them from the genuine historical realities that result from archival research and the use of ancillary academic tools.

The earliest churches presumably date from the time of the rechristianization of Malta in the twelfth and thirteenth centuries after the long Islamic period, between 870 and c. 1240 when the island was an essentially Muslim enclave. One of the first securely recorded churches was oddly enough that of Santa Maria, on the little rock of Comino, which gets a mention in a portolan composed around 1296. This and other churches, including several rock-cut ones, could have been Greek-rite establishments set up by Sicilian Basilian monks who, as elsewhere in the central Mediterranean, including the Lipari Islands, took the lead in the fight against Islam. Their presence is borne out by the fact that most of the churches bore dedications to eastern or oriental saints, such as St. Basil, or St Catherine of Alexandria. Moreover the churches follow the Sicilian Basilian prototype and are of seminal importance to the understanding of subsequent architectural developments in Maltese church architecture. The fifteenth and sixteenth centuries experienced a boom in church building and by 1575 there were more than four hundred churches to cater for a population that hardly reached the 20,000 mark.

This astonishing quantity is difficult to explain especially since many of the churches bore identical dedications. My suggestion is that many of them had an origin as *ex voto* establishments. Most were privately owned and the founders reserved the right of burial for themselves and their descendants. There were naturally burthens and obligations such as the celebration of masses, or the singing of vespers, on feasts and other specific days when the sanctuary lamp had also to be lit. Proprietors were also expected to properly maintain the building, provide *icone* or devotional paintings, and appoint rectors when so required.

The energy in church building continued unabated in the seventeenth and eighteenth centuries. It was indeed during this period that the most architecturally significant among them were built. The informed patronage of both the Knights of St John and the native aristocracy made itself felt in the choice of the best available *capomastri* (master masons), *scalpellini* (stone carvers), and painters whose combined efforts produced little gems of the type of *Ta' l-Abbandunati* (Ħaż- Żebbuġ), or San Bert (Żurrieq). The nineteenth century saw a decline but the churches that were built, particularly in the second half of the century, are often of notable interest. The more important, in an architectural sense, are those in the Neo-Gothic idiom fashionable in the last decades of the century. Among them those of the Virgin of Lourdes (Għajn Sielem, Gozo), and St. Joseph (St. George's Bay, Bir-Żebbuġa), stand out as notable examples.

The nineteenth century also witnessed an interest in the history of these small devotional buildings which reached a climax in 1866 with the publication of Achille Ferres's informed descriptions. This study remains, to date, the most authoritative and complete work on the subject.

Michael Spiteri, affectionately known as 'Kilin' is, in many ways, the twentieth century's most worthy successor of Achille Ferris and the simple, easy going style of his beautiful Maltese and English prose writing, which appeals to a wider audience, has stimulated greater interest in their preservation and continued existence. I am one of the many who acknowledge a debt of gratitude to Kilin for making me love the Maltese small churches and appreciate their charm and historical associations. I remember with nostalgia the short articles which he published in the 1960s in the Maltese weekly *Leħen is-Sewwa* and the way they fired me with an enthusiastic response to an aspect of the Maltese heritage which was later to become a major academic preoccupation. Kilin has now honoured me with the invitation to write the preface to the second edition of his most important book on the subject. This has given me great joy.

Mario Buhagiar
The Art Unit, Faculty of Architecture,
University of Malta

NOTES

1   The architectural meaning of *kappella* (chapel) is a part of a church
    which is set apart for private or special worship or, sometimes,
    a small liturgical building physically linked to the main body of
    a larger church. It is never an independent building. In the
    Maltese mediaeval context *capella* stood for parish church e.g.
    cappella di Bir Miftuħ, or *cappella di Santa Caterina* (Żejtun). The
    word *kappillan* (parish priest) means "he who looks after the
    cappella (i.e. parish church).
2   A.T. Luttrell, "Girolamo Manduca and Gian Francesco Abela:
    Tradition and Invention in Maltese Historiography", *Melita
    Historica vii/2 (1977), 105 - 132.*

FOREWORD
TO THE FIRST EDITION

Visitors to these islands may be struck by the large number of churches to be seen both in the towns and villages as well as dotted around the countryside. Those of the locals who have never been abroad may not be aware of this peculiarity of the Maltese environment.

On the two main islands there are hundreds of churches, ranging from the monumental, like St. John's Co-Cathedral and the Mosta and Paola temples, to quite tiny chapels. I propose to call attention to just one hundred of the smaller ones.

Why are churches so numerous and so ubiquitous on the Maltese islands? One reason is undoubtedly the religiosity of the people. Another may be the fact that in the past, when the population was made up mainly of peasants and the roads were bad, every little hamlet sought to have its own church. A third reason is that in many cases the chapels were built in fulfilment of vows.

Soon after the re-christianisation of Malta after the long Arab period, little chapels appeared all over the islands. The square-mile islet of Kemmuna has its church, built of rough-hewn stones, and there was one even on the bare rock of Filfla. In most cases the churches had cemeteries beside them.

One comes upon the chapels in the most unlikely spots, like the cliff of San Dimitri in Gozo's "far west", or tucked away under rocky outcrops in valleys, like those of Wied il-Ghasel, Wied Gherxija, and Gozo's Wied il-Lunzjata. Some add sharpness to the outline of hills. Others form part of the houses of the nobility. Villages have grown around some of them, while others, like those of Bir Miftuħ and Ħal Millieri, once centres of thriving communities, now stand alone in the fields.

No two are exactly alike. While falling broadly within known architectural orders, from the troglodytic to the ultra-modern, each church has its own individual character, with some interesting variations of detail. One, for instance, will have a bell-cot growing out of the pediment; another a quaint lozenge-shaped window; a third, a horse' trough beside it.

Taken individually each little church is something lovely and precious in one colour, as a garnet, or an onyx, is precious. But look at them collectively, and suddenly it is as if each individual gem were a tiny stone set in an old Roman mosaic. There springs to life a picture of the islands' past: the wars, the hit-and-run raids by corsair or Turk, the plague and cholera epidemics, the famines and droughts, the pageant of rulers from various countries, the unfolding of art and architecture through the centuries, and the devout faith, as well as the superstitions, customs and folk-lore of the common people who form the hard, permanent core of the tiny but hardy nation.

Having been the centre of village life for centuries, it is not surprising that many stories, legends, traditions and quaint customs should be intimately connected with the chapels. At least one is said to be haunted. A certain cross or statue in another chapel commemorates a miraculous deliverance from the plague. In a third you may see a painting of the Madonna which was slashed by Napoleonic bayonets. In yet another you may be shown a statuette that used to be lowered in the sea along with fishing nets as a silent prayer for a good catch. A Turkish cannon-ball in another is a relic of the Great Siege of 1565. Several churches still bear the scars of bomb splinters of the second world war.

Regrettably, during recent decades the churches and chapels have been sadly neglected, and in more than one case advantage was taken of their isolation to rob them of artistic treasures ranging from Mattia Preti paintings to humble ex-votos. A few chapels, notably those of San Pawl Eremita of Wied il-Ghasel and Santa Maria tal-Virtù, fared even worse, failing victims to a vandalism which can only be described as diabolical. One sincerely hopes that with the nascent interest in the conservation of the environment greater care will be taken of what is left, if not the restoration of what has been lost.

The information contained in this book is far from being a complete treatise on the churches included here. For deeper historical study the archives of the public library and those of the Cathedral Museum, and the several learned books on the subject, are indicated. The best sources of all are the reports of the Pastoral Visits carried out at regular intervals by the Bishops, where the state of the churches is described in detail. I hope that this book, the work of an amateur, may serve to whet the appetite of those who have the time and the inclination to delve deeper into the subject.

A word about the sketches. I have redrawn, at leisure, those done twenty years ago, often in a great hurry so as to meet the deadline of a weekly article in *Leħen is-Sewwa*. So don't be surprised if you find changes, such as a missing bell or a cross that has been knocked down and never replaced, or if a block of flats has been built obstructing the view and dwarfing a chapel. On the other hand you may be delighted to observe that certain chapels have been cleaned, while others like San Gwann t'Għuxa, San Pawl Milqi, and San Mikiel is-Sanċier, have been restored by loving hands.

KILIN
1990

THE BEGINNING

It is the year 60 A.D. A grain ship on its way to Rome is caught in a terrible north-easter and, after drifting helplessly for fourteen days and nights, is wrecked on the island of Malta. Miraculously, not one of the two hundred and seventy-six souls on board is lost. One of them, Luke, will later leave us a detailed account of the voyage in chapters 27 and 28 of the Acts of the Apostles. The greatest day in Malta's history has dawned, for Paul the Apostle has brought the Good News to the islands.

Luke goes on to describe how the survivors were welcomed and the loving care lavished on them by the "barbarian" islanders who could not understand how the deadly bite of a viper had no effect on Paul. Publius, the chief man of the island, received the shivering survivors in his house and treated them most generously for three days.

1. San Pawl Milqi – Burmarrad

Where was the house, large enough to receive the crowd of survivors? Was it where the church of San Pawl Milqi now stands? The adjective "milqi" might mean "welcomed". Bishop Molina (1630) states that according to a very old tradition it was on this spot that Paul and Publius met. The church of San Pawl Milqi stands on a hill called Ġebel Għawżara, near Bur Marrad. It is not the first one to be built on the site. The area has been known by various names:

Burmarrad, Buwarrad, Beniarrat, Benwarrat and Bindiki, or Pintiki.

In 1372 King Federick IV of Aragon granted to Giacomo de Peregrino the fief of Beniarrat, qualified as being "venerable".

In the list of benefices granted by Bishop de Mello in 1436, that of San Pawl Milqi is described as being "of ancient foundation".

By will in the acts of notary Luigi Sillato, dated 28th March, 1448, some land was bequeathed to the church of San Pawl of Bindiki.

The name Milqi is first mentioned in the report of the Pastoral Visit of Bishop Cagliares in 1616.

Cagliares stated in his report that on the day of the feast of St. Paul, thirty-six measures of wheat and thirty-six of wine of Syracuse (some 28 litres), two hundred cucumbers and nine tari (money) were distributed to the poor. Among those who contributed were the Knights of St. John of Jerusalem.

According to Bishop Molina the owners of the fields adjacent to the church were under the obligation to pay twelve scudi a year to the procurator for the celebration of Masses on the feast of St. Paul, those of obligation, and on Sundays.

The present church was built in the seventeenth century. During the 1914-18 war Royal Engineers digging a trench nearby uncovered massive walls, but no importance was attached to the find, in spite of the fact that since the eighteenth century it had been known that the site had archaeological importance. Dun Karm Gauci, who had charge of the church collected and preserved many potsherds turned up by the ploughshares in the vicinity.

In 1964 an Italian Archaeological Mission excavating at San Pawl Milqi, both around and inside the chapel, uncovered an extensive complex comprising a country villa, oil and wine presses, and accommodation for many farm labourers. They dug so deep that the church door is now some three metres above ground level.

The owner must have been a very wealthy man. It is believed that the complex was built around the year 40 B.C. and that it was still in use in the year 870 A.D. when the Aglabite Arabs occupied Malta.

Considering the extent of the farm-cum-villa it is possible that this is where the Apostle and his fellow-survivors spent their first three days on the island.

But similar villas existed at Wardija, Bidnija and Għajn Tuffieħa, and it is believed that while Publius met Paul and welcomed him at Bindiki, it was in Wardija that he was given shelter.

The Museum Department, together with the Cathedral Chapter, had plans to house in this area a small permanent exhibition of all the objects discovered on the site. An excellent idea which one hopes will some day materialise. The church which had suffered severe damage from vandals, has been restored.

2. St. John the Baptist
"Tal-Ħereb" – Wardija

In chapter 28 of the Acts of the Apostles, Luke relates how Paul prayed and laid his hands on Publius' father, who was prostrated with fever and dysentery, and cured him. Whereupon the sick from all over the island were brought to Paul and all were cured. It is not surprising that according to an old tradition many were baptised on the spot. Cornelius a Lapide mentions this tradition in his commentary on the Acts. In the early seventeenth century the Maltese Jesuit Gerolamo Manduca proposed that it was in the neighbourhood of this chuch that St. Paul stayed three days with Publius immediately after the shipwreck. A large stone bowl, or trough, situated near another chapel not far from St. John's is reputed to be the font used by the Apostle.

Manduca stated that he saw the remains of many Roman buildings on Wardija hill, at the spot called "Tal-Ħereb", which means "the ruins".

In his Pastoral Visit of 1617, Bishop Cagliares reported that an older church existing on the site of the present one had been deconsecrated but rebuilt in 1610 by Gerolamo Xerri of Naxxar who endowed it with the rent of a field which had been given to him by the Grand Master. The church already enjoyed the rent of two scudi from another field.

The church was rebuilt completely by Count Nicola Sciberras Bologna, owner of those lands, in 1852. Bishop Cocco Palmeri, who loved to spend his leisure time at this spot, engraved his coat of arms on the wall of the contiguous villa.

During the 1939-45 war, the villa, in which the gunners manning the guns nearby were billeted, was bombed, but the church was not hit. The house was rebuilt by the Meli Bugeja family, who bought it from Count Dun Franġisk Teuma Castelletti, who lived in it before the war.

On Sundays during the summer months Mass is celebrated at St. John's.

THE CAVE CHURCHES
AND CATACOMBS

St. Luke has left on record that St. Paul and those shipwrecked with him stayed in Malta three months. They could not do otherwise because at that time navigation in the Mediterranean was prohibited by law during the three months of winter, the ban being lifted on the 5th March with a feast in honour of the Egyptian goddess Isis.

The wealthy Publius, grateful for the healing of his father, would certainly have wished to play host to Paul until he sailed. But Paul was not a man to stay idle for any length of time. The love of Christ urged him relentlessly to lose no time or opportunity for the preaching of the Good News. So, after three days, off he went to Melita, the capital of the island.

The city, which was later to be renamed Mdina by the Arabs and reduced in size for purposes of defence, extended beyond the present perimeter for about two kilometres into the suburb of Rabat. The moat outside the walls on the *southern side stretched from the present Ta' Saura hospice to Bir-ir-riebu.*

Beyond the ditch, as far away as where the Dominican church now stands, there was an extensive burial area. I remember how, in the thirties, when trenches were sunk to lay the foundations for new houses, more often than not Punic burial chambers were uncovered. Early in the christian era catacombs were dug in the same area.

Halfway along the ditch, and just beyond it, there existed a cave. According to a strong and constant tradition St. Paul stayed in it. Presumably, citizens whom he had healed would have been only too glad to receive him in their homes. But Paul's independent disposition is well known from his epistles where, again and again, he insists that he did not want to be a burden on anyone.

According to the same tradition he used to enter the city where, close to the main gate, he raised the cross and preached the Risen Christ.

St. Paul's grotto is reputed to be the first church on the island.

3. The Penitent Magdalen – Rabat

St. Paul's cave, attracted pilgrims from the Christian world, as did Jerusalem, Rome and Santiago de Compostela. Since early times many faithful, both Maltese and foreign, wished to be buried as close as possible to Paul's cave, even in the ditch itself. The Parish church of St. Paul, described in old documents as "St. Paul outside the walls", straddles the ditch, and from it a stairway leads down into the cave. Beside the church is a fairly large churchyard, called "Zuntier". (As we shall meet with this word again, it is well to note that in many cases it has come to mean the space close to a church, or "parvis") Within the boundaries of the Rabat Zuntier there rises a mound on which, according to a popular tradition, Paul preached, his words being heard in far-off Gozo! A statue marks the spot.

Many tiny chapels once existed in the Zuntier. The Penitent Magdalen, dating from the third century A.D., is the only survivor. Its entrance is only a few paces from the side door of the Parish Church. It was built in the late nineteenth century in a style that recalls a funerary chapel. The door leads straight down a stairway to an underground church.

Two circular stone tablets, depicting St. Paul and St. Peter, once located in this crypt, are now exhibited in the Parish Museum. On the left-hand side of the stairway is a passage leading to two fairly large rooms excavated in the rock. At the bottom of the stairway is the semi-circular chapel, also dug out of the rock, with an altar surmounted by a stone relief. A ledge three feet wide and eighteen inches high runs round the wall. At the centre of the dome-shaped ceiling of the crypt is a hole, similar to a well-shaft, on top of which, above ground, is a small cupola.

On the right side of the chapel is a passage leading to a niche holding a statue of Our Lady "Tal-Ħlas", protectress of women in labour. A shorter passage on the opposite side twists to the left and opens out into a smaller chapel with an altar. The passage then narrows again to end in a narrow stairway which climbs to the Zuntier surface close to the mound and statue mentioned above.

The relief of St. Mary Magdalen, the work of Giovanni Bonnici replaced a painting which was damaged by damp. The statue of Our Lady "Tal-Ħlas" is of recent date, the work of the late sculptor Marco Montebello (1915- 1988). It replaces a statue of Our Lady of Lourdes, now preserved in the church sacristy.

Up to ninety years ago the underground chapel of the Penitent Magdalen was forgotten and neglected. Parish Priest Dun Carmelo Sammut (God rest his soul! He baptised me) took an interest in it. What had happened before that? In the report of the pastoral visit of Monsignor Pietro Dusina (1575) we read: "he visited the subterranean burial place at Rabat, close to the church of St. Paul, excavated in the rock, in a hallowed place, which is reached by means of a stairway. There is a stone altar, and it is a decent place." But he added: "some building stone lying there should be removed, and a wooden door should be provided to keep people out." In the said manuscript there is mention of eleven other chapels, all deconsecrated by him.

It has been suggested that the church was recut from the *tullianum*, a Greek-style prison of Roman Melita where the apostle could have been detained during his stay in Malta. Such a theory is, however, unsupported by the archaeological and textual evidence. On the other hand there are indications that the church might have been recut from an early Christian catacomb at an unknown period in the late middle ages. This was, in fact, a major cemeterial area in Punico-Hellenistic, Roman and Byzantine times. Other churches at Rabat, such as Santa Maria tal-Virtù and the Virgin of the Grotto were similarly recut from late Roman tombs.

Independently of the Magdalen chapel, the presumed prisons are of considerable interest. In one of them one can see the loops cut in the stone to which the more intractable criminals were bound. (Were Paul and Silas so bound in the inner prison at Philippi? Acts. 19, 24)

The prisons have not been completely investigated. Some believe that they are connected with the catacombs.

Behind the statue of Our Lady "tal-Ħlas" is a wall blocking yet another corridor. Where does this lead to? Another prison chamber, perhaps, or a passage to the city? When, and if, excavations are made, the ground under the church of St. Paul and the zuntier may yet prove a precious hidden and forgotten history-book of the early church in Malta.

During the 1939-45 war the Magdalen chapel served as a bomb shelter. Sterling work of cleaning and preservation was carried out by the late Dun Vinċenz Galea. Later the Environment Division of the Education Department cleaned another part of the crypt.

4. St. Cataldus – Rabat

The Catacombs are only a short distance from St. Paul's Parish church of Rabat. Three of them, St. Paul's, St. Agatha's and St. Cataldus' are clustered together. One kilometre away are the Tad-Dejr Catacombs. The nearest to St. Paul's Grotto is St. Cataldus'. It is the smallest of the four but none the less interesting, as some of the graves of the canopied or baldachino type, are in the form of a four-poster double bed. Others are wall niches known as arcosolia. There is also an "agape" table, a round low platform with raised rim, at which relatives and friends of the deceased partook of a "love" meal.

Above the catacombs a crypt was hewn out of the rock and served as a chapel, as happened in other places such as St. Paul's grotto and St. Agatha's crypt. Traces of frescoes are still visible in the catacombs and deserve to be conserved and protected.

Above the crypt a free-standing church was erected. Mons. Dusina deconsecrated it in the year 1575. Devotion to the saint, an Irishman who was bishop of Taranto, was strong in the sixteenth and seventeenth centuries. It is recorded, in a will dated 1595, that Notary Mario Mallia and his heirs left moneys to pay for the singing of first vespers and the celebration of a sung Mass on the 10th May, feastday of the saint, and for keeping the lamp alight.

The church was demolished in 1739 but rebuilt in the present enlarged form in 1745. A fine altar painting of the saint in Bishop's robes is signed by Antoine Favray. In the church there is a wooden statue of the Immaculate Conception, and a stone statue of St. Cataldus graces the square in front of the church.

Until some years ago, on the occasion of the "festa", the pulpit used to be brought out onto the tiny parvis, and the sermon used to be called "the leaven of Corpus Christi", as it was in a way considered to be the prelude to the feast of Corpus, held at the parish church in June, always with great solemnity.

Another very old custom, discontinued a few years ago, was the holding of a market of farm implements near the church on Sunday mornings.

5. The Mellieħa Sanctuary

According to a very old tradition the highly venerated sanctuary of the Nativity of Our Lady of Mellieħa was blessed by St. Paul the Apostle. The same tradition would have it that the icon of our Lady painted on the bare rock is the work of St. Luke the Evangelist; a theory supported by Mons. Pirri (1630), Ġan Franġisk Abela, Giacomo Bosio, Count G.A. Ciantar and Mons. O. Bres. On the contrary, Mario Buhagiar wrote that it is "Byzantinesque in inspiration but Sicilian or South

Italian in execution, (and) datable to the late thirteenth or early fourteenth centuries." *(The Iconography of the Maltese Islands)*

That it has enjoyed the great devotion of the Maltese people is evidenced by the large number of ex-votos and other offerings.

A number of bishops appear in the painting on the sanctuary ceiling. It is believed that they represent seven bishops who according to a pious legend visited the cave sanctuary while on their way to a Council at Milevo, near Carthage, in the year 416. Seven crosses painted on the walls are claimed, on no evidence, to indicate that these seven bishops consecrated the cave. Similarly unfounded is the story that Augustinian friars looked after the sanctuary in 420 AD.

Important visitors are said to have included King Ferdinand IV (1373), King Martin (1408), King Alfonso (1432), Viceroy Lupo Ximénez (1468), Ferdinand d'Acuña (1490), and much later Bishop Lavigerie, Nicola Speciale, and St. Benedict Joseph Labre, who was visiting the Marian sanctuaries of Europe.

In 1436, Mellieħa was one of the ten parishes mentioned in the financial report presented to Bishop Senatore de Mello. It extended as far as Mosta. However, as Mellieħa was exposed too much to the frequent attacks of Turks and pirates, in 1551 it was annexed to the parish of Naxxar. In 1614 the invaders sacked the Mellieħa sanctuary. Bishop Balaguer, writing some forty years later, recounted how one of the attackers, on recovering from a serious illness which he considered to be a punishment for his part in the raid, sent a votive candle to the sanctuary.

During the Great Siege, Don García de Toledo, who landed his relieving force at Mellieħa Bay, visited the sanctuary on the 7th September. Since that day it came to be known as the church of the Nativity of Our Lady, popularly known as "il-Vitorja".

Ten years later, when Mgr. Dusina visited the sanctuary, he found it without a rector, without any income, and quite bare. It was still rectorless in 1587 when Bishop Gargallo visited it, and so it remained till the year 1603 when he appointed Dun Bernard Cassar to the post.

The year 1614 saw the Turkish attack mentioned above, after which Grand Master Alof de Wignacourt began to visit the sanctuary regularly on Saturdays.

The Brotherhood of the Holy Rosary was formed in 1669. In 1690 Mario de Vasi, of Syracuse, enlarged and embellished the church, placed a statue in the lower crypt, built a house for the rector and rest-rooms for pilgrims.

The church was enlarged further and consecrated by bishop Alpheran de Bussan on 21st. May 1747. In 1834 Mellieħa became a vice-parish, and in 1844 Bishop Caruana again raised it to the status of parish, following the grant of a bull by Pope Gregory XVI. The first parish priest was Dun Pawl le Brun. The building of the new parish church started in 1883. By decree of Pope Leo XIII the miraculous icon was crowned on the 24th September, 1899, by Bishop Pietru Pace, assisted by the Bishop of Gozo, Mgr. G.M. Camilleri.

In recent years the sanctuary has been extensively decorated, the walls being covered with marble. There are now five altars, and paintings of Our Lady of Carmel, St. Andrew and St. Paul. Canon Dun Vicenz Grech Delicata donated to the sanctuary the relics of St. Vincent, martyr, brought from the Cemetery of Priscilla in Rome on the 21 st April, 1920. Popes John XXIII and Paul VI have honoured the sanctuary. Pope John Paul II prayed in the sanctuary on the 26th May. 1990.

Many have been the graces obtained through the intercession of Our Lady, those of rain after periods of severe drought being particularly remembered. A national pilgrimage which took place in 1718 is commemorated by the arch erected outside the church. Another national pilgrimage, this time during a cholera epidemic, was in 1888 led by the Apostolic Administrator, Mgr. A.M. Buhagiar.

6. Our Lady "Tal-Virtù" – Rabat

Driving uphill from Attard to Mdina one sees the bastions of the city merging with the buildings of Rabat. On the far left rises the Hotel Verdala, and beside it the Archbishop's Seminary. A kilometre farther out the dome of Our Lady tal-Virtù rises from a grove of dark-green pine and carob trees.

The church is built on an important archaeological site, a cemetery with punic, hellenistic and late roman tombs, and a catacombal complex or palaeochristian hypogeum, about which the historians G.F. Abela and

A.A. Caruana wrote a description. The latter wrote that the catacomb was blocked, but later, in 1901, he could gain access to it and found that the catacomb had been converted into a crypt, in late mediaeval times, with a gothic door engraved with acanthus leaves.

The church was already built in 1436 because that year a certain Antonio de Bigliera bequeathed in its favour the rent derived from a small tract of arable land. (Acts of Notary Luigi Sillato). The church was rectangular, had an arched roof, and an apse. In Mgr. Dusina's report it is said that it had three altars and a stone bench.

In 1674 Abela wrote that the walls were covered with intonaco to carry frescoes similar to those found in other mediaeval churches. It also had an icon, painted on wood, which was later replaced by an alabaster statue of Our Lady of Trapani.

The altar-piece was a painting of Our Lady with Child, done in 1611 by Vincenzo Baiata, mentioned in the pastoral visit of bishop Cagliares, (1615). It has now been transferred to the Wignacourt Museum in Rabat.

The present church was built between 1717 and 1723 by Petruzzo Debono. The sculpture of the beautiful altar is by Benedetto Saliba, who was helped by Antonio Fabri.

The church enjoyed great devotion. There was a time when the walls were literally covered with ex-votos. The Archpriest of the Cathedral used to go to Tal-Virtù in procession on the second Sunday after Easter, and bless the four winds. This was called the "feast of the buds and blossoms". Pilgrimages were made in times of national calamity, such as droughts and earthquakes.

Pope Leo XIII declared the twentieth century the century of the Redeemer. In conformity with this, the Bishop of Malta, Mgr. P. Pace, and a committee convened for the purpose, caused an imposing statue, cast in iron, of Christ the Redeemer, holding a large cross and with the right arm raised in benediction, to be hoisted to the top of Tal-Virtù dome, facing north. To make it a truly national gesture, every family on the island was asked to contribute one penny. On the 22nd September, 1901 the statue was escorted to Rabat by a detachment of the Royal Malta Artillery. A speech was delivered by the Chief Justice, P. Debono, and poems were read, one of them by a young priest, Dun Karm Psaila, later to be acclaimed Malta's national poet. Two large commemorative plaques were uncovered.

In September 1923 an earthquake, which I distinctly recall, caused serious fissures to appear in the dome. The church was in a dangerous state and was closed to the public.

The statue was lowered in 1935 and placed on a stone pedestal close to the entrance to the drive leading to the church. The cross was blown away in a bad storm, and the place became sadly neglected. In 1986 the statue was renovated and transferred, pedestal and all, to the grounds of the Seminary.

In recent years the church itself was horribly vandalised, the door being knocked down, the walls disfigured with irreverent paintings, the altar damaged, and the whole place filled with rubbish. Happily, in March, 1988 at the request of lovers of Malta's heritage, the Department of the Environment did some sterling work of cleaning and renovation.

It is not surprising that legends and ghost stories
should be connected with this old church. The most
common is the following:

A certain priest, called Dun Bernard noted for the
holy life he led, used to say Mass in Tal Virtù church.
A short time after this priest died, a farmer who had
climbed from the valley to go to hear the 4 a.m. Mass,
(called the Aurora Mass) at St. Paul's, met a priest
near Tal-Virtù who invited him to serve Mass. The
farmer did so. The priest thanked him and told him
that that same day he, the priest, was going to
heaven and would pray for him.

According to another version the farmer did not
know how to serve Mass, but helped by handling
the missal, bell and cruets without saying the
responses. At the "lavabo" he froze in terror on
seeing that there was no flesh on the priest's hands.
Towards the end of Mass, when the priest consumed
the holy species, the farmer ran away. At the door
he glanced back, only to see that the priest had
vanished. When he related what had befallen him
he was not believed, but those who decided to go
and check the story found that there were plain signs
on the altar that Mass had indeed been offered.

During the 1939/45 war one of the soldiers
quartered in the church related a similar experience,
claiming that he had been wakened by a priest who
asked him to serve Mass. Again the bony fingers
were in evidence, and again the scared soldier was
gently asked to carry on serving Mass. Then the
priest walked straight through the locked door and
vanished.

Yet another legend relates how the Dominican

fathers, the back windows of whose convent overlook the road from Rabat to the chapel, once saw a devout maiden, just dead, accompanied by her guardian angel, proceeding to Tal Virtù. The young lady, sister of the renowned sculptor Melchior Gafà and his equally famed brother, the architect Lorenzo, was very fond of praying in this chapel.

Legends. Believe them or not …

7. Our Lady "Tal-Minsija" – San Ġwann

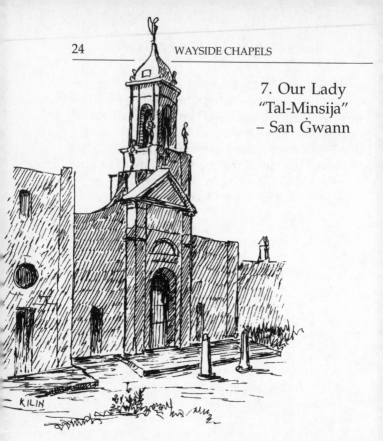

KILIN

Il-Minsija means "the forgotten". The name is derived from an old tradition, according to which at some time in the fifteenth century a certain peasant named Andrew, who was digging in his field, saw a light shining through a crack in the rocky ground. On digging deeper he uncovered a cave in which was a niche containing a painting of the Madonna, and hanging in front of it a candelabrum with three lights burning. Forthwith he reported the find to the Parish Priest of Birkirkara. The latter decided to remove the painting and keep it at his residence. Next day it was back in the cave. Again the priest took it home, and again it was found back in the cave. He reported the case to the Bishop who took the painting to his palace. And yet once more it was found in the cave. The Bishop then ordered the clearing of the debris which had accumulated in the cave, and the building of a stone altar. The entrance to the cave was closed by an iron grating. The tradition finds some corroboration in the pastoral visitation reports, but the discovery of the painting took place in the late seventeenth century. The name of the farmer is not known.

The present painting in the cave is a triptych showing St. Leonard in the centre, flanked by the Archangel Gabriel and Our Lady in the volets. It is the work of a fifteenth, or early sixteenth century vernacular artist who was probably Sicilian.

After its discovery the cave chapel was neglected. It was deconsecrated in 1645, and again in 1659, but was reopened during the time when Cocco Palmeri was Bishop (1681-1711), when two rooms were built near it for the keeping of the sacred vestments and to be used by the priest. Devotion to Our Lady became very strong, especially after the cure of a lame man who, by way of thanks, built a lodge for visiting pilgrims.

Around the year 1877 a priest from Birkirkara, Dun Ġorġ Debono, took up residence beside the chapel, which he paved taking with him his sixteen-year old nephew, Michael. He used to say Mass daily.

Pope Leo XIII, on the 20th December, 1879, declared the altar a privileged one. When Michael

Debono grew up, he built the present church, but did not touch the cave.

On the 1st July, 1911 Bishop Peter Paul Pace granted an indulgence of one hundred days to whoever recited an Ave Maria at Tal-Mensija. A statue of the Assumption was placed on a pedestal in front of the church.

Directly one enters the door of the chapel a deep stairway leads down to the cave. At its sides are statues of the twelve apostles and, opposite, one of Our Lady of Lourdes. In the cave there are two altars, one dedicated to Our Lady and the other to Christ the Saviour. Besides other paintings there is a Via Crucis.

The Capuchin Fathers of San Gwann Parish say Mass at Tal-Minsija, and celebrate the feast of St. Leonard.

8. The Immaculate Conception – Msida

KILIN

This very old church is affectionately called "the little church" by the Msidians. It is situated in the older and poorer quarter of the town. It has a small zuntier with a statue of the Immaculate Conception on its left side.

A door cut in the rock leads to a smaller chapel which has an altar dedicated to Our Lady of Carmel. Beyond this is the small sacristy. Behind the main altar is a statue of the Immaculate Conception, a thanksgiving offer of Antonio Famucelli after the plague outbreak of 1675/76, known for some reason as "the plague of Mattew Bonnici". The church has two bells. In Mgr. Dusina's report of 1575 this chapel is said to have been dedicated to Our Lady of Succour. It was enlarged in 1640, and again thirty years later. A great benefactor of the church was Fra Filippo Wolfgang Von Guttenberg, Bailiff of Brandenburg, who left moneys for its improvement and endowed it with rents. This knight had a house reportedly not far from the Ghajn tal-Ħasselin, the covered public washing place still to be seen in Msida Valley Road. A tablet in the chapel testifies that he left a foundation for the celebration of Masses on Sundays and Festas. Dionisius Famucelli, a renowned silversmith and father of Antonio, who was procurator of the church, built the sacristy.

In 1835 the church became a vice-parish church. In 1859 it was repaired. On the 2nd March, 1867, as the population had grown considerably, Bishop Gaetano Pace Forno raised Msida to the status of parish, the first parish-priest being Dun Salv Caruana. The "little church" served as parish church until the year 1891 when the church of St. Joseph was built. The old church was then neglected and fell into disrepair. But in 1916, following an appeal for funds made by the Auxiliary Bishop Fr. Angelo Portelli, O.P. repairs and structural modifications were carried out. Already, in 1910, Parish Priest Schembri had rebuilt the facade.

The paintings at the sides of the main altar, representing the Flight into Egypt and our Lady of Sorrows, have been restored. Mass is celebrated daily in the church which has been well redecorated. It is used for spiritual exercises and retreats.

A number of theories exist about the origin of the church. Undoubtedly it is very old. The original small chapel was dug in the rock, as many old churches were. According to legend seven maidens took refuge in the cave when pursued by Turkish raiders. The Turks saw an apparition of Our Lady and fled screaming "Omm Sidna" (Our Lord's Mother). This, according to some is the origin of the name Msida. But it has been observed that several places in Malta have the prefix "M". (Mġarr, Mtaħlep, Mnajdra, etc.) The late Luret Cutajar was of the opinion that the origin of the name was "Għam Sajda", the fishermen's dwelling.

9. St. Lucy – Mtarfa

The church was built in 1500 by the Darmanin family of Birgu. It was visited by Mgr. Dusina in 1575. It overlooks Wied il-Qlejgħa, one of the most charming of Malta's valleys, and the view from the "zuntier" is really pleasing.

Dun Mikiel Saliba, its rector, enlarged it some years ago by opening up the sacristy to create an extra wing. An old staircase was demolished to make place for the new sacristy. In the process an old semi-circular crypt came to light. It had been ruined when stone was quarried from it to be used in the building of the church. Below stairs Fr. Saliba found sackfuls of mouldering *ex votos*, most of which were quite decayed. On some of them the years 1911 and 1917 were clearly decipherable. Fr. Saliba was told that during the 1914-1918 war, when the Mtarfa military hospital was the main one on the island, many of the war wounded were suffering eye damage from poison gas. The *ex votos* presumably were offered by them to St. Lucy, traditionally considered to be the protectress of those suffering from eye disease.

The painting of St. Lucy is very old. Mgr. Depiro, who was later to found the Missionary Society of St. Paul, crowned it during a solemn ceremony. (The "mustard seed" sown by Mgr Depiro has grown into a mighty tree spreading its branches as far apart as Australia, Perú, Canada and Pakistan. The headquarters of the Society are at another historical church, St. Agatha's, in Rabat.)

Under Fr. Saliba's rectorship Mass was said on Sundays and the children of the neighbourhood were taught the catechism at St. Lucy's. In October Mass was said daily and the Rosary was recited.

Except on the feast day, the 13th of December, when the Parish Priest of Rabat leads the service, the chapel is no longer used for services, as the Mtarfa area is now served by the chapel of St. Oswald in the ex-hospital, to which chapel the *ex votos* which could be saved have been transferred.

10. Our Lady of the Visitation
"Ta' Wejda" – Mosta

The church of the Visitation was built, not far from the Cumbo tower, in 1605 by Damiano Bonnici, nicknamed "Wejda". Before it there existed another one, and before that, according to old tradition and as reported by Dusina (1575), there was yet another, dug out of the rock, dedicated to the Madonna, which had been consecrated by seven bishops who had excaped death from drowning only to die in Malta of the plague.

Who were these Bishops? Where were they going when caught in the storm? Were they going to some council in North Africa, or returning therefrom? Could they have been on the way back from a crusade to the Holy Land? It was on such a crusade that St. Louis, King of France died of the plague in 1270. Many crusaders, among them several bishops who had landed in Gozo died of the plague and were according to tradition buried at Tomb Square, Victoria, close to the Augustinian church and convent.

It is possible that the tradition may be founded on fact, and that the seven bishops had visited Malta some time in the late Middle Ages. It could well be, also, that the cave church was one of the subterranean chapels of the pre-Knights' period, like those at Mellieha, St. Paul's Grotto and Tal-Virtù of Rabat.

So, where is the cave? No one knows. It was thought that it was under the present church, but nothing was discovered when excavations were carried out some ninety years ago. It was said that the road between the church and Torri Cumbo used to resound when heavily laden carts passed over it, and this gave rise to the belief that the cave-chapel had been covered over to prevent desecration from the Arabs. A bit far-fetched. Again in that case, the chapel would have been much older than the seven bishops' visit.

A claim similar to Ta' Wejda's, regarding the cave-chapel blessed by seven bishops, has been made for the cave under the church of Our Lady of Good Hope, also in Mosta.

The present church, then, was built in 1610 by Damiano Bonnici. (Cagliares report of 1615). But in the sacristy there is a painting, allegedly done by Damiano himself and dated 1605 showing him and his family venerating the Madonna.

At the time the Rotunda of Mosta was being built, Parish Priest Dun Ġammari Schembri obtained the permission of the Holy See to transfer to the new church all the revenues of the smaller churches of the village. The procurator of "Ta'Wejda" managed to retain the right to one bottle of oil for each field belonging to the church. The rent derived therefrom would today amount to fifteen cents!

"Ta' Wejda", situated quite close to Ta'Qali which during the war was a military airfield, was hit by a German bomb on the 11th March, 1942. It was repaired two years later, when the bell-cot was added. This is commemorated by a tablet above the door.

This church was never deconsecrated, and has been well cared for by rectors and voluntary workers. Sterling work lasting well over fifty years was done by a certain Karmnu Debattista, nicknamed "ta' Xenku". Dun Anġ Dingli, served the church for over thirty years.

Among the works done after the war is the painting of the titular by G.M. Caruana, showing Our Lady singing the Magnificat, and a statue of the Visitation by Wistin Camilleri with statuettes symbolising Faith, Hope and Charity. Fortyfive years ago the sacristy was built and the "zuntier" was paved. Then a gallery for the harmonium was built. A new altar was blessed by Archpriest Dun Bert Bezzina on 17th June, 1964. In 1965 the ceiling was decorated with paintings of Abraham, Moses, David and John the Baptist. Below them appear Rebecca, Sarah, Joel, Deborah, Ruth, Esther, Judith, the verses of the Magnificat, the four Evangelists, and Marian symbols.

The church is very well kept and has all that is required for the divine service. Oil paintings of the Assumption and the Annunciation are at the sides of the altar, which is surmounted by a picture of the Saviour.

The feast is held on the first Sunday after the 11th October, with a sung Mass, vespers and a sermon.

11 The Annunciation – Salini, Burmarrad.

Not far from the Kennedy Grove and exactly opposite the salt storage sheds at Salini, there is this church dedicated to the Annunciation of Our Lady. Until some years ago it had only a few houses near it. Tall and rather ugly buildings have now hemmed it in.

It was built towards the beginning of the sixteenth century, and was held in great reverence by our forefathers. Close by are early Christian tombs.

In the past it lay within the parochial limits of Naxxar and every year the people of that village, led by the Parish Priest, used to go in procession to Salini on the feast of the Ascension in fulfilment of a vow. The Parish Priest used to celebrate Mass and deliver a sermon. The procession was discontinued long ago. According to Bishop Molina (1680) vespers were sung on the feast day, and a free breakfast was offered to all present. The heirs of Giuseppe Buhagiar bound themselves to light the lamp on Saturdays. (*Acts of Notary Ġan Dumink Debono.*) For a long time the Jesuits looked after the church.

"Il-Lunzjata" now falls within the boundaries of the newly-created Parish of Burmarrad, cared for by the Franciscan Conventual Fathers. The Friars have paved the church, removed the side altars, one of which was dedicated to the Apostles Philip and James, installed a "table" altar, and added a confessional. They celebrate the festa, and on Saturdays, at 5 p.m. Mass is celebrated.

The fine titular painting is by the late Chev. Emvin Cremona.

THE HERMITS

In the course of Church history, particularly during the early centuries but continuing right down to our time, there have been those who decided to retire to desert places where, in complete solitude, they sought to escape the daily temptations and distractions of city life and dedicate themselves to meditation and prayer. When numbers of solitary hermits began to live together, the monastic orders came into being.

12. St. Paul the Hermit
Wied il-Għasel – Mosta

"Wied-il-Għasel" means "Valley of honey". But the enchantment of its silence and seclusion are gone for ever. New buidlings overhang the steep sides and, lower down, the horrible quarries and stone crushers provide spalls and gravel to be used in the building orgy which is slowly but inexorably eating up the limited open spaces of the island. Destruction did not spare the chapel of St. Paul the Hermit, which is ensconced in a large cave in one of the rocky sides of the valley. Deeper into the cave is a smaller cave where water trickles into a basin, fashioned by nature, which overflows into another basin, and this into a third before flowing away into the valley. At the far end of the larger cave is a well.

In his description of the chapel Achille Ferres (1866) quotes Father Pelagius as follows:

A pious hermit lived in this cave in which through his miraculous intervention, water trickled. The people of the vicinity led a very wicked life. The hermit repeatedly admonished them. When they would not listen he decided to depart from the valley. Followed by the jeering rabble he went to the seashore. There, after prophesying dire punishment on the island, he spread his cloak on the water, stepped on it, and was carried away to Gozo, paying no heed to the calls of the repentant Maltese. In Gozo he went to live beside the church of the Conception of Qala, where later on he died and was buried, his grave held in great veneration, as reported by the Canon Agius in his Gozo Illustrato. There have been others, however, who believe that this servant of God was the blessed Corrado whose grave is venerated in Noto (Sicily). It is also said that he left his staff here (at Mosta) and on the day dedicated to St. Paul, the first hermit, this staff put out leaves, to the great admiration of those who saw it.

The people of Mosta built a small chapel inside the cave where the hermit had lived and dedicated it to St. Paul the Hermit.

That is the legend. Now for some history:

In 1656 Ġan Pawl Mangion of Mosta placed in the inner cave a painting of Our Lady. It showed the Madonna and Child, the souls in Purgatory, and angels bearing a crown. Bishop Balaguer, on 27th January, 1656, authorised Ġan Pawl to transform the cave into a small chapel by cutting a rude altar out of the rock and placing the picture on it. Mangion had donated funds for the lighting of the lamp on Saturdays and for the celebration of Mass on the feast of the Purification of Our Lady. (*Acts of Notary John Paul Fenech of 28th - 30th December, 1655*). If for some reason the feast could not be held on that day it would be held on the 8th September. The water basin was enclosed in an iron grille and the faithful, among them the Grand Master himself, used to dip into it with great devotion, as is done today at Lourdes.

After the plague of 1676 Dun Ortensio Bennini, "Maestro di cappella" at St. John's in Valletta, used to organise a Mass, with music and a sermon, on the feast day. Among the Grandmasters who venerated Our Lady of Graces of Wied-il-Għasel was Manuel Pinto. But devotion waned when the church of Our Lady of Good Hope was built, as the latter could be reached much more easily.

In 1918, Paċikk Muscat began to look after the Wied-il-Għasel chapel. In 1920 Archbishop Dom Maurus Caruana directed Dun Karm Gauci to do all that was necessary to revive devotion at St. Paul's. Dun Karm built a marble altar, paved the floor, covered the "zuntier" with cement, and surrounded it with an iron railing. He opened a side door and repaired the pathway leading to the chapel. From the well, where the British soldiers of the nearby fort had dumped them, he raised the statuettes of hermit saints (John the Baptist, Paul and Anthony the Abbot) which had been donated by the Bailiff of

Brandenburg, the Knight Wolfgang Philip Von Guttenberg.

Dun Karm used to celebrate Mass on Wednesdays, and open the chapel for visitors on Sunday afternoons. The boys of the Mosta Oratory, who used to accompany Dun Karm for Mass, carried down tiles for the pavement. This was the chapel's happiest period, for it boasted benches, a sculptured stone altar and a small bell-cot. The barrel-vaulted roof was painted. A marble plaque commemorating J.P. Mangion's foundation was affixed to a wall.

Then came the bad times.

When the British engineers opened a passage leading to the ammunition stores not far from the chapel, the material they cut fell onto the pathway used by the faithful to go to St. Paul's, and obliterated it. After that, boys began to climb down the rock face onto the chapel roof, enter the church and leave the doors open. They did not do any damage, but as a precaution it was deemed prudent to remove the sacred vestments to the church of St. Anthony the Abbot, while Mgr. Buhagiar caused the benches to be taken to the church of St. Andrew.

Then came the vandals! They demolished the bell-cot and most of the altar; shattered the marble of the Madonna altar; destroyed the marble plaque; pulled out the iron railing; bashed in the two doors; dumped the statuettes back into the well, together with a lot of rubbish; slashed the pictures of the Madonna and of St.Paul, and scratched obscene graffiti on the walls. Diabolical! To complete the destruction, a rock fell from the roof of the cave, damaged the zuntier and destroyed the path. That was some thirty years ago. An attempt was subsequently made to restore the chapel, and windows and doors were repaired. But again, a rock fell through the roof of the chapel.

Mons. M. Gonzi deconsecrated the chapel during his last pastoral visit.

Fortunately the Madonna picture was carefully restored by the painter R. Bonnici Calì and now hangs in the sacristy of the Rotunda together with that of St. Paul. Copies were later painted by George Apap. The church itself has since been restored by a group of dedicated volunteers, blessed, and reopened for worship on the 12th September 1993. The Saint's feast is celebrated on the first Sunday after the 15th January. In September the feast of Our Lady of Graces, is also celebrated.

13. Saint Mary – Kemmuna

This very old church, built of undressed stones, is situated in St. Mary's Bay. Its old age may be deduced from its shape. Seen from the front it seems to have a flat roof, similar to that of the traditional maltese farmhouse. But inside, the roof rises to a point. The right side and the left meet in a line which begins near the door and ends at the apse. The apse is rounded but likewise narrows to a point in the roof, exactly at the end of the said line.

The painting of the Flight to Egypt shows the influence of Francesco Zahra, but is a mediocre work.

It was restored in 1928 by Chev. Vincenzo Bonello. An old chalice dates from the time of the Knights of St. John.

It is not known when the church was built. What is known is that it forms part of the diocese of Gozo; that it was deconsecrated in 1667 by Bishop Bueno but again opened for public worship by Bishop Cannavés in 1716.

Nearer our time, Mgr. Gonzi used to preach the Lenten Spiritual Exercises at Kemmuna, when he was Bishop of Gozo. Today it is part of the parish of Għajnsielem. The festa is held on a free Sunday in July.

Legend: A holy hermit lived on Kemmuna island at the time that the other hermit, Kerrew, stayed at the Immaculate Conception church of Qala. (q.v.) They used to visit each other, crossing the Gozo channel on their cloaks.

The Barcelona Messiah: Another legend is about the Spanish Jew, Abraham ben Samwel Abdulafia, who, after studying philosophy at Capua went to Spain and declared himself the Messiah. Arrested in Rome in 1280 he was imprisoned in Sicily. On being released he had to flee to Kemmuna to escape the wrath of the people.

Another connection with Qala: When the sea was so rough that the priest could not cross to Kemmuna to say Mass, the inhabitants of the islet used to congregate at St. Mary's bay and, across the intervening channel, assist at the Mass celebrated in the small chapel of the Immaculate Conception known as "ta' fuq il-blat" (above the rocks), which overlooks Ħondoq ir-Rummien.

An archaeological find, close to the church, made in 1912 by Sir Temi Zammit, Director of the Museum, consisted in a human skeleton lying at a depth of one metre on a bed of sand under a layer of red soil. It was covered by two halves of a large earthenware jar.

14. The Immaculate Conception
– Qala, Gozo

This sanctuary is very old. It has been said that it was once a pagan temple.

In 1575, during his pastoral visit, Mgr. Dusina found it in such a bad state of repair that he deconsecrated it. Its property passed to the mother church situated in the citadel of Rabat, (Victoria). Included in the property were lands bequeathed by the noble Ugolino Navarra and Donna Gusmana Navarra.

It was not long before the church was reconsecrated, because in 1591 it was mentioned by

Bishop Gargallo. According to legend it was up to this time dedicated to the Assumption of the Virgin. As the mother church is also dedicated to the Assumption, the people of Qala complained that they could never enjoy their festa properly as it coincided with that in the capital. Accordingly, in 1615 Bishop Cagliares donated to the Qala church a painting of the Immaculate Conception done by a painter close to Federico Barocci of Urbino, (1535 - 1612) and changed the name of the church.

Up to the year 1644, on the day of the festa there was the custom of distributing among the poor as much bread as could be made from the wheat harvested from six "tmien" of land. (The "tomna" is roughly equivalent to 0.278 of an acre). This custom was stopped by Bishop Balaguer Camarasa who enlarged the church and whose coat of arms appears above the main altar.

By 1688 the population of Gozo had grown considerably, and Bishop Cocco Palmeri accordingly created four new parishes: Xaghra, Sannat, Żebbuġ and Nadur. As the only church fit to serve the parish of Nadur was the Conception church in nearby Qala, this church served as a provisional parish church for the two villages.

When, shortly afterwards the new church of Nadur was built, the Conception church was relieved of that service. But on the 1st May, 1855 it was again raised to the status of vice- parish with Dun Anton Camilleri as vice parish-priest.

Around the year 1800 devotion to the sanctuary diminished considerably. But in 1823 Bishop Grech Delicata uncovered a painting of Our Lady with the

title "Salus Infirmorum", done by Pietro Gagliardi
and invited the whole diocese of Gozo to join in a
pilgrimage to earn indulgences granted by Pope Pius
IX. The Gozitans responded with great fervour and
many graces were obtained.

In 1872 the village of Qala became a parish, and
after a short time the new church of St. Joseph was
built and became the parish church.

In 1887 Dun Gusepp Diacono, the Parish Priest,
built the bell-tower of the Conception Church. One
of the old bells is now in Nadur. Another bell which
had cracked was melted down and recast by Julian
Cauchi.

On August 1st, 1954, the main painting was
crowned by Bishop Pace. Mass is celebrated every
day and confessions are heard.

Through the years many pilgrimages were made
to this sanctuary by both Gozitans and Maltese. The
year 1904 is considered a record year. The sacristy,
built in 1762 with contributions made by fishermen
and sailors, was always full of votive offerings such
as pictures, ropes and life-saving equipment, and
crutches. These "ex votos" are mentioned by Bishop
Alpheran (1736) and Bishop Rull (1760). On the
outside of the church one can still see graffiti of
sailing ships, perhaps indicating deliverance from
drowning.

There are three marble altars, the main one being
finely sculptured. The side altars are dedicated to
the Crucifix and to Our Lady of the Rosary. There is
a painting by R. Bonnici Calì. Really beautiful is a
delicately gilded statue of the Immaculate
Conception, after the Murillo painting. Indeed, of all

the country churches, the Qala sanctuary is one of the most tastefully decorated.

In the parish church of Qala is conserved an altar front made of leather and bearing the image of a Madonna and Child which formerly belonged to the Immaculate Conception church. This altar front has been exhibited in London.

Flanking the chapel is an old graveyard.

Legends:

It is recounted that it was at first intended to build this church at a place called tas-Salib, where the village cross now stands. But every morning the building stones left near the cross were found where the church stands today.

The Hermits:

Several hermits are said to have lived in this hallowed place. One of them named James was passing on his way back from a pilgrimage to the Holy Land. He stopped at Gozo and died there. He was buried near the chapel. This happened around the year 990 according to the written testimony of Fra Aurelio Axiaq who had visited this place to exorcise possessed persons. Another hermit was the Servant of God Fra Antonio de San Carlo who led a very saintly life, and died at Borgia in 1726. A third was the Servant of God, Girgor Buttigieg, who is buried in the basilica of St. George in Victoria.

Most celebrated of all is the hermit Korrew, known also as Kurraw or Sirrew. According to an old tradition this is the hermit who used to live in the chapel of St.Paul the Hermit, which is built right under a rock in Mosta's Wied il-Ghasel. (q.v.) At Kemmuna he visited another hermit and then proceeded on his way to Qala where he took up his abode in a cave beside the sanctuary. The said cave, which was then outside the church is now under the building.

When Korrew died people thronged to his grave and many graces were obtained. There was a custom of lowering seriously ill children down a hole in the ground adjacent to the grave, the mothers meanwhile intoning a touching prayer beseeching the holy man to restore the child to health.

It is said that while the mothers were praying the children often saw a man robed in white emerge from the wall, stroke their heads and then return the way he came.

From this same hole the faithful used to take dust which they believed had miraculous properties.

On the exterior of the chapel wall a small cross was engraved to mark the spot under which the hermit's grave was believed to lie. On 19th September, 1937, Dun Ġużepp Vella started excavations to try and find the grave. It was uncovered on the 26th September, right under the base of the wall. On 3rd October a skeleton came to light. It was covered with a layer of fine dust and lay in a reclining position. On the 10th October it was declared that the skeleton was of the fourteenth century, which according to tradition was the time when the Wied il-Ghasel hermit lived. Today one can go down into the cave by means of a staircase.

A very popular festa is held on the 8th December.

15. The Annunciation – Rabat

KILIN

T he old church of the Annunciation and the
Carmelite convent are situated about one mile
from Rabat, and overlook the Wied ta' Liemu valley.
  A church dedicated to the Annunciation was
already in existence on this site before the fourteenth
century. We know this because the noble Donna
Margherita D'Aragona, widow of Giacomo di
Pellegrino, stated in her will in the acts of Notary
Antonio Azzopardo, dated 5th June 1418, that she
left the church of the Annunciation, (*which she had*

rebuilt), to friars, or those who undertook to recite the divine office every day in the said church. To pay for the needs of the church she left all her possessions in the Santu Leonardu area, and other buildings in Gozo and in Mdina.

The executors of the will gave the church to the Carmelite friars who came to Malta some time between the years 1418 and 1452. The name of the Wied ta' Liemu valley below the church is probably a corruption of the name of one of the first priors, Fra Guglielmo Cassar.

Another benefactress of the convent was the noble lady Caterina Sillato who bequeathed to it all her property, by will in the acts of Notary Brandano Caxaro, dated 23rd June, 1562.

In the year 1659 the Carmelites moved to Mdina where Bishop Balaguer Camarasa had given them the church of the Virgin Mary of the Rock. They changed its name to that of the Annunciation in commemoration of their first church.

The old church, abandoned by the friars, suffered considerable damage. In 1662 stones were removed from the convent to be used in the building of the Mdina convent. The violent earthquake of 1693 did not help matters. Repairs were undertaken in 1714 and 1747. In the various attempts to repair the damage the church underwent various modifications. In 1844 the friars decided to restore the church and that part of the convent which was still standing. The front part of the church was demolished to create a "zuntier". As the roof was damaged, supporting walls were built inside and a new roof constructed on them, blocking the arch above the altar and turning the choir into a sacristy. This work strengthened the building but changed its character. The old walls had on the inside graceful recesses in imitation of the gothic style. These recesses were blocked by the retaining walls. In them there were altars. There were at one time many friars, and more than one Mass could be said simultaneously.

The wall built for strengthening the roof is behind the altar. The original altar was on the other side of the wall, under the first archway of what is now the sacristy.

The friars of the old convent were at first buried in a common charnel-house under the choir floor. The cemetery, situated about two hundred metres down the hillside began to be used at a later date. (This was recently renovated, but immediately vandalised.)

A marble plaque on the sacristy wall marks the place where the heart of Grand Master Claude de la Sengle is buried.

On the stone altar there was until quite recently a painting of Our Lady of Carmel, from the workshop of Mattia Preti. Below it was a smaller painting of the Annunciation. The two paintings have now been moved to the sacristy, their place being taken by a fine XVII century painting of the Annunciation. There are in the church other paintings of Carmelite saints, a Via Crucis and a statuette of the Ecce Homo.

In front of the church is a field about fifty metres wide. Beyond and below that field is a cave which is reached by going down a steep flight of stairs. This is a rock-cut chapel older than the first

Annunciation Church. According to Rocco Pirri, Carmelite hermits, around the year 1200, used a grotto as a chapel dedicated to St. Leonard of Limoges, two miles outside Mdina, in a wooded area.

In 1636 Com. Atrea wrote that there was a rock-hewn chapel, close to a spring of water, under the convent. There is a saying that St. Leonard lived for a time in this cave. The neighbouring fields are known as Ta' San Lunard. St. Leonard lived as a hermit about the end of the fifth century, and is considered the protector of slaves, for which reason he was greatly venerated in the Maltese islands, which for centuries suffered grieviously from the frequent incursions of Barbary corsairs.

The cave, or crypt, is semi-circular like that of the Penitent Magdalen chapel of Rabat. In both chapels there is a bench cut in the rock at the sides. On a small altar, set in an apse, stands a statuette of St. Leonard, holding a chain. The statuette, up to a few years ago, was kept in the Annunciation church. On the right side of the crypt is a badly damaged mural showing St. Leonard. It is similar in many ways to another one, also of St. Leonard, in the crypt of St. Agatha's, Rabat, and similar also to the frescoes found at Hal Millieri. Below the cave is the spring mentioned by Atrea.

When I visited this cave thirty years ago it was being used to store manure. It has now been properly cleaned and is used by prayer groups.

Following a very old custom the Carmelite friars go to the Annunciation church on the 5th of November, sleep at the convent, and the following day, feast of St. Leonard, celebrate a sung Mass and the office of the dead. Walnuts were in the past distributed to all who took part in the ceremony.

Another old custom was for the Cathedral chapter to go in procession from Mdina to the Annunciation church where a conventual Mass was celebrated, attended by the Mdina Magistrate.

Both the church and the convent have recently been carefully restored. The convent has been rebuilt on the original plan, and is intended to be used as a house of retreats. A friar and a lay brother now reside at the Annunciation where Mass is said daily at 4 p.m. Frequently prayer groups meet at this quiet and peaceful place.

The Annunciation, most probably the first Marian sanctuary in the Rabat area, which had lain dormant for centuries, has woken up to vigorous life.

EARLY MEDIEVAL
CHURCHES

16. Saint Michael, "Is-Sanċier" – Rabat

This is one of the oldest chapels still standing in its original form. It is low and squat, partly built of rough-hewn stones. Its shape is identical with the late mediaeval style found at Mdina, Bir Miftuħ, Ħal Millieri, etc. The narrow slit window, could have served as a sundial, seeing that the chapel faces west.

The chapel can be seen on the right when going down the road from Rabat to Fiddien. To reach it take the road leading to Chadwick Lake and when it branches to the left follow the signposts down a path enjoying right of way.

San Mikiel is located in an archaeological zone which has yielded thousands of shreds of punic, roman and mediaeval pottery. Architecturally it is dated round the middle of the fifteenth century, with two buttresses added later.

The oldest written document mentioning it, is Dusina's Pastoral Visit of 1575. It refers to it as the church of St. Michael in the garden of Ġnien is-Sultan. In 1678 Bishop Molina deconsecrated the church and ordered the painting of St. Michael to be transferred to the parish church of St. Paul in Rabat.

The chapel has been used by farmers as a store for tools and manure, and as a cow-shed. Two brothers, built a wall to divide the chapel into two sections, each one having a door.

In 1981 a group of volunteers known as the Sanċir Trust, with a lot of voluntary work and funds provided by the National Students Travel Foundation and the Friends of Malta removed this rubble wall and restored the church.

Like many other old chapels San Mikiel has its legends. One of them is that pigs housed in it sickened and died, while cattle grew fat and yielded milk in plenty.

I confess that in my "Wayside Chapels" I called the chapel St. Demetrius or St. Cyrus. St. Demetrius was in fact another small chapel in nearby Ġnien Fieres. St. Michael stands in the area called Ġnien is-Sultan. For some unknown reason St. Michael is called San Mikiel is-Sanċier. This led to the opinion that the church is dedicated to Saint Cyrus. There seems to be no documentary proof in support of this theory.

17. The Annunciation – Gozo

Nestling picturesquely under a rocky crag this church looks down on the fertile and well-irrigated valley that bears its name: Wied il-Lunzjata. It can be reached by the road from Tomb Square, Victoria, past the church of St. Augustine, or by following the left arm at the bifurcation of the Victoria-Kerċem road, or from the village of Kerċem itself.

It is one of the oldest of our churches, probably dating from the time of the islands' liberation from the Arabs. It is first referred to in the "statutes" of Martin, king of Sicily from which we learn that it was a "juspatronatus" founded by Doña Sibila of Aragón in the year 1347. When Doña Sibila died leaving no heirs, the juspatronatus passed to the kings of Sicily as rulers of Malta.

Those were troubled times, full of political and ecclesiastical tensions. Pirates from North Africa frequently swooped on the islands in sudden raids, pillaging and carrying off the inhabitants into slavery. The practice of piracy, however, was by no means one-sided. There were times when the booty captured by Maltese corsairs constituted the main source of the islands' finances. The Maltese did not hesitate to attack Greek and Christian ships. In 1371 they attacked a Genoese vessel. The reprisal was swift and terrible as a naval force under Thomas Murchio sacked the islands.

The following year, King Frederick IV of Aragon visited Malta to see what could be done to repair the damage, and at the same time to strengthen the wavering loyalty of the Maltese. He visited the Lunzjata chapel and exercised his right of juspatronatus by nominating Dun Bartolomew Axiaq as its rector.

In 1398 King Martin, the Younger, granted the benefice to a Maltese priest, Sagona, and in 1472 Viceroy Don Lope Ximénez de Urrea granted it to cleric Gerolamo Tabone.

In 1501, Dun Pietro de Beniamin, the rector, was carried off into slavery. Viceroy Acuña trasferred the benefice to Alvaro del Castello, but the latter was similarly enslaved.

In 1530 the Knights of St. John of Jerusalem took possession of the islands. Grand Master D'Homedes granted the benefice to Dun Peter Burlò.

In 1629 the chapel was rebuilt by Dun Paul Tabone, the rector, who commissioned a painting by the artist Garagona.

In 1644, the rector, Dr. Nicola Mangion, paid for an altar-piece painted by Fra Luca Garnier. Mangion's coat of arms appeared on the stone altar.

A small sacristy was built in the year 1700 by the rector, Dr. Ercole Martino Testaferrata.

There is today a small organ gallery and a lovely statue of the Annunciation by the late gozitan sculptor Wistin Camilleri. A marble altar, taken from St. Sabina church in Victoria, has replaced the older stone one.

The chapel was consecrated by Mgr. Giuseppe Pace, Bishop of Gozo, on the 18th October, 1959.

18. The Annunciation – Ħal Millieri

KILIN

Ħal Millieri, which is within the parochial limits of Żurrieq, is today uninhabited, the only buildings visible, being two old chapels. The many wells found in the area, however, indicate that it was much different in the past. In 1575 Mgr. Dusina reported that there were at Ħal Millieri fifteen houses and no less than four churches, namely: the Annunciation, the adjacent Visitation, St. Michael and St. John the Evangelist. The two still standing are the Annunciation and St. John's.

Up to some thirty-five years ago both were neglected. Mr. Luret Cutajar wrote repeatedly to the papers about the need to restore certain historical chapels, among them the "Sanċir" chapel of Rabat and the Annunciation of Ħal Millieri. Regrettably the no less important Santa Duminka of Żabbar had been destroyed during the war.

Luret was particularly insistent on the importance of saving Ħal Millieri, even offering to defray the cost of repairing the roof which was in danger of collapsing. And he was by no means a wealthy man. His appeals fell on deaf ears. But following the appearance of a series of articles of mine in *Leħen is-Sewwa*, people began to wake up to the idea of the importance of the smaller churches.

(I take no credit for this, as there was nothing original in the information I furnished. Probably it was the sketch that did it.) Anyway, the newly-founded Youths Section of Din l-Art Ħelwa, under the direction of Mario Buhagiar and George Serracino Inglott, began to clean the church removing a mountain of rubbish and rubble in the process. The Żurrieq Civic Council gave a helping hand.

A veritable treasure came to light in the shape of a number of frescoes which provided a link between the Siculo-Byzantine and the Renaissance periods. They represent the Saints Nicholas, Andrew, George, James the Elder, Lawrence, Vincent the Martyr, Paul, Augustine, Blaise, Agatha and Leonard. Some time in the past someone had actually whitewashed them, maybe when the chapel, like that of Sanċir, was used as a stable. Fortunately it was not too late to have them restored. The restoration was undertaken in

1978 by Paolo Zanolini of Milan, and the following year the medieval specialist Dr. Anthony Luttrell edited a book of specialised studies on the church.

Books have since been written about Ħal Millieri. Excavations, carried out by A. Luttrell, Tom Blagg and Tony Bonanno, and the late Director of the Museums, Francis Mallia, uncovered the foundations of an earlier church, which also had been decorated with frescoes.

The Annunciation is built in the later medieval style. The square door appears to have been originally ogival, as above it are the remains of a drip-mould similar to those at Bir Miftuh. The roof rests on four pointed arches. At floor level there are stone benches between the arches. The old altar, which did not accord with the style of the church, has been removed and a simple table altar installed instead.

At the time of the Dusina visit, the Annunciation was in a good state of repair, was paved and had three altars. But there was no rector, sacred vestments, or any income. Dusina ordered that the side altars were not to be used during religious functions. They were in fact removed.

The church was after this neglected and at some time deconsecrated. But a certain Ġużè Magro restored it, and it was blessed by Dun. Gaetano Buttigieg, delegate of the Bishop Ferdinando Mattei on 6th November, 1809. But it was again neglected, and by the time Luret Cutajar drew attention to it had nearly collapsed.

19. St. John the Evangelist – Ħal Millieri

St. John's is only a few paces away from the Annunciation church. It is one of the twelve churches dedicated to the Apostles which once formed a ring around the village of Żurrieq.

In 1575 Bishop Dusina found that it had stone benches, a floor of beaten earth, but no doors. A peasant called James Mifsud used to pay for the celebration of Mass on the feast day. Dusina deconsecrated the church, but it was later reconsecrated and equipped for religious service.

Again it fell into disrepair until, some seventy years ago, a mastermason, Mikelanġ Coleiro of Żurrieq, took it in hand. While clearing up the field behind the chapel he uncovered chasubles and other vestments which were buried in the soil. Coleiro, repaired the church properly, built an altar, and caused the titular painting to be restored. After the church was reopened he continued to look after it, making sure that the feast day was well celebrated. After he died his grandchildren continued the good work.

But once again, the chapel was neglected, until it was again overhauled at the time the Annunciation church was being restored.

At the time I drew the sketch, thirty years ago, the cross atop the column on the right had been shot away by "sportsmen" who practiced their markmanship on it. It was replaced.

The stone font on the "zuntier" is interesting. It seems to be the remains of an olive pipper of the Roman period similar to those kept at the Museum of Roman Antiquities (Rabat) and the Cathedral Museum.

20. St. Mary of Birmiftuħ – Gudja

Birmiftuħ was one of the ten parishes mentioned in the 1436 report of Bishop Senatore de Mello. From it later there branched out seven new parishes, namely: Gudja, Luqa, Tarxien, Kirkop, Mqabba, Safi and Ħal Farruġ.

It is believed that the church of the Assumption of Bir Miftuh existed some time in the late Middle Ages long before it became a parish church The present church was originally bigger. Of the six doors only two remain, three being walled up while of the fourth only a half remains, the other half having been cut off when the church was reduced in size.

It is also believed that other churches existed alongside Santa Maria. They were dedicated to the Assumption, the Birth of Our Lady, St. Sebastian, St. George and St. Catherine. All these have disappeared. The church was reduced to its present size in 1512.

When the Knights of St. John of Jerusalem came to Malta in 1530 they nominated a captain for the defence of the area of Bir Miftuħ.

The Apostolic Delegate, Mgr. Dusina (1575) found that the church was well equipped for the divine service. He found two altars flanking the main one. As both were dedicated to the Assumption of Our Lady, he caused them to be removed. Finding that the Blessed Sacrament was kept in a cupboard on the altar he ordered the construction of a gilded wooden tabernacle. The dead were at that time buried in a pit in the middle of the church. Dusina ordered that proper graves be dug.

The church was attacked on more than one occasion by Moslem raiders. It is recounted that the treasures were hastily buried in a grave, or according to another version, thrown down a well, and that they are still buried, along with the old bells. It is the old fable of buried treasure, similar to that of the golden calf allegedly buried in various parts of Malta and Gozo, or that of the treasures of the Alhambra, hastily buried by the Moors just before their expulsion from Spain in 1492.

Around the year 1655 the people of Gudja decided to build a new parish church, because Bir

Miftuħ was too exposed to attack. Everything was
transferred to the new church. Among other objects
there was an old porcelain basin, bearing a design
of the Baptism of Christ, which was used for
christenings.

On the 24th of January, 1663, unknown persons
broke into the church, ransacked the place, forced
the door of the tabernacle and made away with a
silver pyx containting consecrated hosts. The
unprecedented   sacrilege   caused   general
consternation, and the Grandmaster, Raphael
Cotoner, and Bishop Balaguer issued a joint
condemnation of the unknown thieves, who were
excommunicated. Then, three days later, the empty
ciborium was found in the confessional of the church
of St. James in Valletta.

The crime was investigated at length by the
Inquisition, but the culprits were never caught. The
case intrigued me, because there are points which even
today are as thought-provoking as a detective story.

There were in Malta at the time no less than three
religious authorities, namely, the Grandmaster, the
Bishop and the Inquisitor. Understandably, all were
keen on catching the culprits. Lesser crimes were
punishable by death. The gates of Valletta were well
guarded. Thus, to enter the city with the stolen pyx,
and moreover to deposit it in a church, was an act
bordering on madness. Who, then, could the culprit
be? Was he someone above suspicion? Why leave
the pyx in a church? And if a church, why not St.
John's, but St. James', a church attended by the
Knights of the Langue of Castille? What happened
to the consecrated hosts?

Basing myself on these questions, and after reading through the lengthy process of the Inquisition, I wrote a novel, "L-Għafrid".

In 1830 baroness "Bettina" Muscat Cassia D'Aurel repaired the church. This was commemorated by a small coat of arms on the wall blocking one of the old doors of the church. It was stolen a few years ago.

The church is built in the late medieval style. The doors are decorated with the peculiar horse-shoe drip-mould appearing on doors of buildings of the period. On the right-hand wall there appears a small Byzantine cross.

The main painting, on wood is believed to date from the late XVI century. Wall paintings depicting the Last Judgement and figures of Saints are also of the same period. They were found just after the last war when repairs were carried out, which uncovered among other things an altar built on columns, gold buckles, rosaries and holy medals.

Important restoration works have recently been undertaken by Din l-Art-Ħelwa, which holds the church in trust.

21. Saint Mary of Ħax-Xluq – Siġġiewi

KILIN

This church, situated just off the road from Siġġiewi to Qrendi, is very old. Siġġiewi is listed in the 1436 De Mello report as one of the original parishes of Malta. It comprised four hamlets: Ħax-Xluq, Ħal Kbir, Ħal Niklusi and Ħal Kdieri. In those hamlets and the surrounding countryside there were many filial chapels. Mgr. Dusina, in 1575, listed no less than forty-six in the Siġġiewi area, six of them in Ħax-Xluq. One of the six was dedicated to the Visitation, one to St. Nicholas, another to St. Agatha, and three were in honour of the Assumption of Our Lady. One of these three was the chapel shown in the sketch.

Ħax-Xluq was the largest of the four hamlets, and St. Mary's was the principal church, where baptisms were celebrated, although the parish church was that dedicated to St. Nicholas of Bari.

In the year 1575 Mgr. Dusina deconsecrated a large number of churches which were not sufficiently well kept. St. Mary's was in a very bad state of repair, and fell under Dusina's axe. But nine years later John Paul Buttigieg rebuilt it, paid for the titular painted on three wooden panels and left a small rent derived from the field Ta' Kobbi for the celebration of Mass on the feast day and for the lighting of the lamp. His son, Dun Stephen, became rector of the church in 1596 and five years later parish priest of Siġġiewi. He was removed from office six years later by order of the Sacred Romana Rota for showing disrespect to the Inquisitor. Shortly afterwards he was pardoned and appointed parish priest of Attard.

In 1615 a certain Anton Dalli bequeathed to the church the rents from two fields. Other foundations included one from Dun Stephen for the celebration of a Mass once a month. Also trasferred to St. Mary's were foundations for Masses enjoyed by the deconsecrated churches of St. Nicholas of Ħax-Xluq, St. Agatha of Bir Ġobrun, the Assumption of Bajdun and the Assumption of Bir Gobrun (Report of Bishop Molina, 1680). At the time the Parish Priest of Siġġiewi celebrated Mass on the feast day, when first vespers were sung. Early this century a band used to play on that day, and toys and "pasturi" (small clay figurines) were for sale close to the church.

The feast is now celebrated on the Sunday following the fifteenth of August. In the past there was the curious custom of preaching a panegyric in honour of St. Roque during the evening Mass. This Saint enjoyed great veneration, being considered a protector against the plague.

Besides the titular painting there are at St. Mary's paintings of Christ before Pilate and carrying the cross, both by one of the painter Zahra's assistants. There are also statues of St. Roque and St. Rita, and a picture of Our Lady of the Holy Rosary.

22. The Saviour – Żejtun

KILIN

Situated in the older part of Zejtun, originally the hamlet of Bisqallin, this church was built in the year 1500, and dedicated to the Visitation of our Lady. The façade was rebuilt in 1749 through public contributions. The name was changed to that of Christ the Saviour, but someone insisted that a statue of Our Lady be placed close to the church.

It is evident that the church was at some time enlarged. The roof of the recess behind the main altar is a barrel vault, while the outer part has pointed arches. It is believed that the recess was the original Visitation chapel but there is no documentary evidence of this. The side walls are buttressed. In the right-hand buttress there are traces of a side door. The original pavement was of limestone slabs. In the inner half of the church there were once many graves. The bones were placed in one grave when the floor was paved with marble in 1952, when Benigno Schiavone was procurator. Among the benefactors who contributed for this pavement was a certain Angela Żammit.

The main altar is of stone. It was retained when a fine new table altar was installed. The two altars at the sides, ensconced between arches, are dedicated to Our Lady of the Rosary and the Sacred Heart. The titular painting is in the style of Francesco Zahra. More recent paintings are by Tusè Busuttil.

Mass is celebrated daily as well as various feasts, including the titular. The Rosary is recited all through October, and the Via Crucis during Lent.

23. The Assumption – Żabbar

It is not known when this church was built, but it is undoubtedly very old. Various modifications have been made to its structure. Under the Greek cross of the front there were two holes in which small bells used to hang. The style of the door does not accord with the rest of the building, and the belfry is only about one hundred years old.

It has been said the church, or rather the apse, had been built in fulfilment of a vow made by a man unjustly charged with murder but subsequently acquitted.

The roof is a barrel vault resting on eight arches. At the inner end the church narrows down to what is little more than an apse, inside which is a stone altar. The titular painting is by R. Bonnici Calì. It substitutes a much older one of Our Lady of Graces in which the Madonna, wearing a silver crown is represented seated, with the Child Jesus holding a globe. Flanking her are St. Paul and St. Leonard of Limoges, while lower down appear a youthful St. John the Baptist and a slave whose broken chains are at his feet. At the top of the picture an angel thrums a harp and another bears a flower garland. This was once the titular painting of the Zabbar sanctuary, and is now kept in the parish museum.

Two paintings, one of the Crucifixion and the other of the Nativity, have also been taken to the museum.

Two rooms at the sides of the apse have recently been amplified and are used for the teaching of the catechism. Above the round skylight is a lantern, but there is no cupola. Above the main door is the organ gallery, but the old organ is no more, a small electric harmonium now providing the music. In the two niches at the sides of the nave are statues of Our Lady of Sorrows and of St. Anthony of Padua.

The feast is celebrated on the 15th August. In the past a breakfast used to be offered to all who took part in the celebration. Mass is said daily.

24. Old Saint Joseph's
– The Citadel, Gozo

This is one of the oldest churches in the Gran Castello, the Citadel of Victoria. It was already built during the Great Siege (1565) but under the name of St. Nicholas.

Mgr. Dusina recorded that the first chapel built inside the Gran Castello was that of St. Lawrence. When, in 1575, he deconsecrated it, the faithful turned to that of St. Nicholas.

Bishop Baldassarre Cagliares (1614-1673), whose mother was a gozitan, altered the lay-out of the church according to a plan by Vittorio Cassar (who had died in 1609), and rededicated it. It was the first church in Gozo to bear the name of St. Joseph. Cagliares built his palace close to it. He left a legacy for the celebration of Mass at St. Joseph's every Saturday.

From 1672 onwards the Chapter of the collegiate church, now the Cathedral of Gozo, used to sing vespers and high Mass on the Saint's feast day.

In 1693 there took place a violent earthquake. The roof of the church fell in. The church was abandoned and suffered further damage. The Chapter discontinued the celebration of the feast and the Cagliares legacy lapsed. The church became a ruin.

Sir Harry Luke, who was appointed Lieutenant Governor of the islands in 1930 dedicated himself to the restoration and conservation of buildings which had a historical value. In the Gozo Citadel he restored Casa Bondì, a veritable jewel, which now houses the Gozo Museum. In 1937 he started work on the Cagliares palace and the adjoining church. Unfortunately his term of office terminated soon after, and the work he had started stopped half way. Still, it can be said that were it not for his work St. Joseph's would today be a heap of rubble. Arches similar to the old ones had been completed and a lot of valuable work done in Cagliares' house.

The historical buildings suffered from neglect and, worse still, vandalism. The refuse of the Cathedral, including the remains of old coffins, was dumped in the palace yard, and whenever the heap of rubbish rose to a certain height it was burnt!

But the 16th August, 1973 was a happy day for Old St. Joseph's. Seminarians Leli Magro, Toni Spiteri,

Ġużeppi and Vitor Vella, together with Dun Tony
Mercieca and a number of altar boys of the Cathedral
tucked up their sleeves and started to clear up tons
of rubbish. After cleaning they began to restore. They
painted doors, glazed windows, scraped the walls,
swabbed the floor. Finding a very old chandelier
which used to hang in the Cathedral, they hung it
in St. Joseph's.

Other people followed the youths' example.
Gozitan sculptor Toni Camilleri, after carefully
examining the remains of the old altar, designed a
new one. The Superior of the Capuchins of Gozo
donated parts of the altar in his church which were
found to fit the new altar. Censu Cordina painted a
new altar piece as the old one had been restored and
hung in the Cathedral Museum. Other anonymous
benefactors chipped in, donating a Via Crucis and
lamps. Mgr. Paul Cauchi gave a pair of old
holy-water stoups, formerly installed in Ta' Savina
church, and a set of candlesticks.

Old St. Joseph's was reopened to the public on
the 19th March, 1975 by Dun Ġużepp Saliba. On that
day the Pope sent a special blessing to the altar-boys
for the work they had done.

On the eve of St. Mary's, 15th August, 1976,
Bishop Nikol Cauchi solemnly blessed the church
and declared it open to the public.

25. Saint John (The Almoner) – Bormla

The Cotonera district, comprising the towns of Birgu, L-Isla and Bormla (also known as Vittoriosa, Senglea and Cospicua) takes its name from the formidable line of fortifications, enclosing the three cities on the landward side, built by Grandmaster Nicola Cotoner in the seventeenth century. The church of San Ġwann t'Għuxa stands just behind the bastion near the end of the line where it abuts on the dockyard, only a short walk away from the Għajn Dwieli tunnel which pierces the fortifications at this point.

The eight-pointed cross of the Knights of St. John of Jerusalem carved above the door might give the impression that the church is dedicated to St. John the Baptist, patron of the Order. It is in fact dedicated to St. John Elemosiniere, "the Almsgiver," born in Cyprus in the year 556 who, on becoming a widower and losing his sons, lived as a hermit in Egypt and for his charitableness and saintly life was appointed Bishop and Patriarch of Alexandria. He died in 619. His feast-day falls on the 23rd January.

The original church built in honour of the Saint was situated about one mile outside the walls of Birgu. Attached to it was a house, with a garden, inhabited by a hermit. An indication of the antiquity of the church can be had from the fact that in the sacristy there was a coat of arms of Antonio Vulpono, or Volpunno, a Benedictine who was consecrated Bishop of Malta by Pope Gregory XI in 1373. Although Bishop of the islands for twenty years Vulpono very rarely came to Malta, preferring to reside in Sicily, presumably because these islands were at the time plagued by frequent incursions by Barbary pirates.

The church of San Ġwann formed part of the parish of Bir Miftuħ, Gudja, from 1436 up to 1592, when it was incorporated in the newly formed parish of Tarxien.

There existed once in this church a wooden statue of St. John the Baptist which, according to the historian Abela had been a figurehead on the Knights' "Caracca" of Rhodes, whilst, according to Agius de Soldanis it was carried on the galleys of the Order. It is now in the chapel of relics in St. John's Co-cathedral.

When Nicola Cotoner erected the fortifications, the church of St. John, which created an obstruction, had to be demolished, but was rebuilt two years later on the present site, the Knight Prior Fra Pietro Viany footing the bill. The year of the rebuilding. 1682, is carved on the door. A house was built next to the church to serve as residence of the Conventual Chaplain. It was from this house that alms were distributed to the poor.

During the first world war St. John's served the spiritual needs of the soldiers stationed nearby. In the second, St. John's, which practically overlooks the dockyard, found itself at the heart of the target area. Scars from bomb splinters can still be seen on the walls. The chaplain's house was hit and was later demolished by the Public Works Department.

Two fine Preti paintings, one depicting the Saint distributing alms to the poor, and another showing God the Father, have been transferred to the National Museum.

Up to the last war meetings and conferences used to held regularly in St. John's, and occasionally Mass was celebrated.

For many years, because of the extensive damage it had suffered, the church was kept closed, the main door barred with planks nailed to it as used to be done during epidemics of the plague. Restoration has been carried out by the Ministry of Culture assisted by a group of students of the Gerolamo Cassar school.

26. Saint Agatha – Mdina

For hundreds of years, Saint Agatha was venerated as a protectress of these islands, together with St. Paul and St. Publius. Above the main gate of Mdina, on the inside is a high relief showing the three saints.

The small church of St. Agatha, contiguous to the monastery of Benedictine Nuns is only a few yards away from the gate, at the first turning left.

It was built in 1417 by the noble Francesco Gatto and his wife Paola de' Castelli, and was a lay juspatronatus of the Gatto Murina family. It reverted to the Church in 1661.

It suffered considerable damage in the violent earthquake of 1693, but was rebuilt a year later by the architect Lorenzo Gafà, the Dean Adriano Bonnici paying the expenses.

Archdeacon Gio Antonio Cauchi blessed it on the 28th June, 1695, in the presence of the Grandmaster, Adrien Wignacourt, and Bishop Cocco Palmeri. The Grandmaster buried medals in the masonry. to commemorate the occasion.

In the titular painting are depicted St. Agatha and St. Adrian, martyr. It was done by Giuseppe d'Arena during the rectorship of Dun Adriano Bonvicino. Another painting, on wood, representing Dun Giuseppe Manduca, done in 1553, is now in the Cathedral Museum.

A small plaque on the door indicates that the Society of St. Vincent de Paul used to hold their meeting here.

27. Saint Mary - Magħtab – Għargħur

This church, dedicated to the Assumption of Our Lady, is not very far from Bahar-iċ-Ċagħak, below the Għargħur cliffs near the cave of San Brankat. It can be reached by a side road which branches from the Naxxar-Salini road.

According to the report of Mgr. Dusina (1575) and Cagliares (1616), it was very old and held in great veneration. It was rebuilt in its present form in the XVII century.

Mass is celebrated on Sundays and on feasts of obligation.

TURKS AND CORSAIRS

For hundreds of years the Mediterranean was the scene of conflict between the Christian South of Europe and the Moslem North Africa. Both sides engaged in hostile operations ranging from hit-and-run raids to full-scale operations like the ill-fated crusade of Louis IX against Tunis in 1270 and the Great Siege of Malta of 1565.

The watch-towers around the coast of Malta, like the string of towers along the south coast of Spain, (Torremolinos, Torrevieja, etc) are grim reminders of the state of anxiety and constant fear in which the inhabitants of these islands lived.

In one of his famous Novelas Ejemplares, Cervantes wrote that one was likely to go to sleep in Tarifa and wake up in Tangier. The same could be said of the Maltese if for Tangier you read Tunis or Tripoli. The victims of the raids were dragged into captivity. Thousands of Christians were enslaved in Turkey and the Barbary states. Literally thousands of Christian galley-slaves were set free *at the battle of Lepanto. On the other hand hundreds of Moslem captives used to sleep in the slave prison in Valletta.*

Both Christians and Moslems collected large sums of money for the ransoming of captives.

28. St. Gregory's – Żejtun

The massive retaining walls of this church give it the appearance of a fortress. Close to it are two cemeteries. On its site there was once an earlier church the pavement of which has been uncovered some eighteen inches below the present one, and whose blocked door still exists.

The area was known as Santa Caterina. because the old church was dedicated to that saint. The period when the church was built is not known. Pope John XXII (1316-34) had ordered that the feast of St.

Catherine, virgin and martyr, was to be celebrated in all the churches of the West. Later, the church came to be popularly known as St. Gregory's because of its association with the annual votive procession.

In 1436, St. Catherine's was one of the ten parishes mentioned in the De Mello report of that year. Its limits included the villages and hamlets of Għaxaq, Marsaxlokk, Żabbar, Gwann, Bisqallin, Bisbut, Tmiem, Ġilwi, Dmikki, and San Ġorġ. The 1492 inscription reported by Abela, now lost, referred to the rebuilding of the church. The transepts were re-roofed in 1593 and 1603. The church was a prebend of the Cathedral Precentor, and coats of arms of several of the incumbents appear on the vestry walls, the oldest being that of Canon Axiaq. It bears the date 1372.

On several occasions the church was attacked by the Turks. Very grave damage was done to it in a particularly fierce attack which took place on the 6th July, 1614, when close to 6,000 Turks landed at Marsaxlokk and laid the countryside waste. Parish priest Dun Mattew Burló had to suspend the administration of the sacraments in this church up to the 11th September.

A painting of St. Gregory was done in 1615 at the request of the Prior of lbernia, Pedro González de Mendoza. One can see on it his coat of arms and that of the city of Mdina. Other paintings are those of St. Catherine and of Our Lady of Carmel. These were originally in the new parish church and were replaced by others. The church began to be called St. Gregory's when the new parish church, also dedicated to St. Catherine, was built.

In 1708, Bishop Cocco Palmeri ordered that the new church of St. Catherine become the parish church of Żejtun. Apparently he intended to minimise the importance of St. Gregory's because he ordered that the traditional procession of St. Gregory should thenceforth end at the new church.

Again during his pastoral visit of 1709 he ordered a reduction in the size of the church by means of the building of a wall under the dome, and the erection of an altar against the said wall, decorated with columns taken from the old altar. He moreover ordered the demolition of the St. James chapel, the sacristy, the side chapels, and the dome. But by the time the sacristy and the choir had been pulled down, his successor, Giacomo Cannavés, rescinded the order that the procession end at the new church.

In 1838 Canon Annetto Casolani commissioned the stone statue of Pope St. Gregory the Great which can be seen beside the church, facing in the direction of the Cathedral. The designer was Giuseppe Hyzler, and the sculptor Salvatore Dimech of Mosta, (incidentally my great-great-grandfather). It was at this time that the buttresses on the side walls of the church were built to strengthen the walls of the nave.

In 1969, workers carrying out repairs to the lower part of the dome came upon a door blocked with masonry. Behind it many human bones were discovered in three narrow corridors.

In 1799-1800 the church was used as a hospital by the Maltese insurgents. During the 1939-45 war it gave shelter to refugees from the Cotonera District, and was later used as a military store.

The St. Gregory votive procession was instituted by Bishop Cubelles early in the sixteenth century. All the parishes of Malta used to take part. Originally the procession used to take place on the 12th March, but as this date nearly always fell during Lent, Bishop Labini in 1781 transferred it to the first Wednesday after Easter. After the procession the participants used to relax in a country feast comparable in popularity with the Mnarja festival of Buskett. This national procession was unfortunately suspended in 1926.

Opinions about the origin of the procession vary. Some have said that it was in thanksgiving for deliverance from an invasion of locusts; other that the deliverance was from the plague. Another claim is that it was for deliverance from a Turkish incursion. In 1575 Mgr. Dusina questioned a number of people about the procession. He was told that it was to commemorate a providential storm which had scattered a large force of Moslem ships which had tried to enter Marsaxlokk Bay.

St. Gregory's is today a sub-parish catering for the religious needs of the people of this part of Żejtun where two large housing estates have gone up.

29. Our Lady of Good Hope – Mosta

KILIN

The church is built above a cave in Wied-il-għasel. According to Ciantar, the historian, the cave is the one described as "the cave of the Visitation" in the report of the Apostolic Delegate Dusina, according to whom it was consecrated by seven Bishops. (See the same claim made in the case of the other Mosta church, Ta' Wejda)

According to a touching legend a Mosta maiden was one day working in the fields of Burmarrad when she saw running in her direction a number of

Turks. With her heart in her mouth the maid ran towards Mosta with the Moslems in hot pursuit. Out of breath she managed to take refuge in a cave the entrance to which was one mass of cobwebs. She prayed fervently to the Madonna for protection. The corsairs looked high and low for her, even peering into the cave, but seeing a veil of *untouched* cobwebs they decided that she could not have gone in there. They gave up the search and, fearing an attack from the village, hastily withdrew. Convinced that it was Our Lady who had helped her escape the girl decided to build a chapel atop the cave.

Building started in August 1760 and the church was completed eleven months later, the procurator being Ġammari Galea.

Built in Renaissance style the church has an octagonal interior. The painting of Our Lady of Good Hope is by Rokku Buhagiar. Other paintings are of the four evangelists.

Three niches adorn the façade. In the middle one is a statue of Our Lady of Good Hope, with the Child Jesus grasping an anchor. In the side niches are statues of St. Joseph and St. Anthony of Padua. Above the side niches are coats of arms, one bearing the monogram of Our Lady and the other those of Bishop Rull in whose time the church was built.

There is a small sacristy where hangs another painting of Our Lady of Good Hope, by Giuseppe Calì. The zuntier in front of the church was enlarged in 1898 through the efforts of Dun Ġwann Fenech. In1913 the same procurator cleaned and renovated the cave, crowned the dome of the chapel with a beautiful lantern designed by master-mason Salvu

Żahra. In 1923, procurator Dun Ġużepp Vella paved the church and the sacristy with marble.

On the 3rd July, 1966 Bishop Galea consecrated a new marble altar, credit for which goes to Dun Karm Dingli.

On either side of the main altar are niches with statues of St. Rita and St. Francis Xavier. There is also a statue of Our Lady of Lourdes.

The days of the Lourdes apparitions are commemorated with Masses. The feast of Our Lady of Good Hope is celebrated on the third Sunday in November. Also commemorated, this time in April, is the feast of Our Lady of Good Counsel.

The cave of the legend is well kept and decorated with many flowerpots and ferns. Above the railing is a stone statue of the Archangel Michael. Inside the cave is a statue of a maiden kneeling in prayer and others of the evengelists Luke and John.

30. St. Paul – Marsalforn, Gozo

KILIN

The present church of St. Paul at Marsalforn is probably the third, if not the fourth, to be built on the site. In the past it enjoyed great devotion, the faithful often walking to it in procession, especially in times of drought.

The historian Canon Agius de Soldanis asserted that the apostle St. Paul visited Gozo, and that the Marsalforn church was built to commemorate the fact. The date of the building of the first church and its cemetery is not known. Mgr. Dusina makes no mention of it in his report dated 1575.

Always according to Agius de Soldanis the church was rebuilt by a certain Cheltres, a governor of Gozo early in the XVII century. According to others the name of the governor was Scipion Graielles Chalettes, and the date of the building was 1641. In 1649 the Knights of St. John had the right to nominate the rector.

In 1663 the church was in such a bad state that Bishop Miguel Balaguer Camarasa ordered its restoration, from the very foundations, the expenses to be defrayed from its own benefices and those of the church of the Assumption at Għajn Meddew in the neighbouring village of Xagħra.

In 1715, during the Grandmastership of Ramón Perellos, a small fort was built around the church, complete with ditch and drawbridge. At that time Malta and Gozo were sorely plagued by raiding corsairs. Once they sacked St. Paul's and among the things carried away was the altar-cloth. On sailing away they were caught in a violent storm. Believing it to be in retribution for the sacrilegious theft, the corsairs returned and put back the cloth.

In 1730 the church was once again in a very bad state, and Dun Mattew Spiteri of Xagħra collected money for the repairs. Again in 1878 the church had fallen into disrepair and Bishop Pietru Pace decided to enlarge it. Government granted a plot of land. (*Acts of Notary Giovanni Refalo*). Antonio Giardina was the architect and Ġużè Vella, of Żebbuġ, the builder. In August 1879 Bishop Pace blessed the church and dedicated it to the Shipwreck of the Apostle. He donated to the London Museum the old altar-piece, reputed to be the work of Sister Maria De Dominicis,

who had worked with Preti in St. John's
Co-Cathedral.

The present altar-piece is by Giuseppe Bonnici.
The painting of the Sacred Heart was done in 1879
by an artist whose name is not recorded. The same
year the capuchin friar GioBatta did the paintings of
the four Evangelists, and those of St. Andrew and
St. Francis Xavier. A good painting of the Sorrowful
Virgin is by Ignazio Cortis. The statue of St. Paul,
blessed by Dun Fortunat Grech on 24th February,
1925 is by Wistin Camilleri. Also by Wistin is the
statue of St. Joseph, done in 1959 during the
rectorship of Dun Salv Sultana.

The mosaic pavement was laid in 1933. The
marble main altar, by Karmenu Micallef was done
in 1938, while the altar of Our Lady of Sorrows, also
in marble, was completed in 1963.

Dun Ġammarì Attard paid for the altars, Francis
Caruana for the statue of St. Joseph, while Judge
Montanaro Gauci paid for the church clock.

As the population of this very popular seaside
resort has grown considerably the church has
recently been enlarged by roofing over the adjoining
yard.

31. Our Lady of Ransom – Qrendi

"Tal-Ħniena" (Our Lady of Ransom) has long been held in great veneration. It was built during an unknown period when the hamlet of Ħal Lew still formed part of Żurrieq. When Żurrieq became a parish, Tal-Ħniena served as vice-parish to serve the people in that outlying area.

In the titular painting appear three figures, thought to be St. Ramón de Peñafort, St. Peter Nolasco, and Jaime Primero, "el conquistador", king of Aragón (1263-1276) who had formed the congregation "De mercede redemptionis captivorum" (the ransom of captives).

In 1575, Tal-Ħniena was in a bad state, and was deconsecrated by Mgr. Dusina. In spite of this the devotion of the faithful continued unabated, and the church was rebuilt in the year 1650 when Dun Ġammarì Camilleri was parish priest of Qrendi. The new parish of Qrendi had been formed on the 15th February, 1618, when Bishop Cagliares dismembered the hamlets of Ħal Lew and Ħal Manin from the parish of Żurrieq.

The large number of "ex voto" paintings the church possesses bear witness to the devotion it enjoyed. Among its many benefactors were Dun Ġammarì Camilleri, John Schembri, and the Bailiff of Brandenburg, Fra Wolfgang von Guttenberg. The coat of arms of the latter appears on various pictures and ornaments, among them a seashell-shaped font.

The sacristy was added in 1668. The painting of St. Magdalen is believed to be a work of the studio of Mattia Preti. That of the crucifix is attributed to Sister Maria de Dominicis, and among the many other paintings are those of the Assumption, by Giuseppe d'Arena, and of St. Anthony of Padua, by Rocco Buhagiar.

On the 18th March, 1695, at the request of Parish Priest Dun Dumink Formosa, indulgences were granted in favour of Tal-Ħniena by Pope Innocent XII. This Parish Priest's zeal was the cause of his death, because in 1699, when the new parish church was being built, to set an example to the parishioners, he climbed a tall ladder carrying a heavy stone, fell, and was killed.

The founder of the Society of Christian Doctrine, the saintly Dun Ġorg Preca, used to assemble his followers at this church on St. Michael's day.

Behind the iron bars of the side windows one can see a hole down which oil for the lamp used to be poured, and also a slot for contributions in coin.

The church has three altars, a wooden organ gallery, a statue of the Redeemer and several paintings. One of the paintings is very interesting as it represents the fourteen "saint protectors" who used to be invoked by the Maltese in cases of sickness and other trials. They are: *St. Blaise*, (throat diseases), *St. George*, (diseases of the skin), *St. Erasmus* (bowels), *St. Pantaleon* (tuberculosis), *St. Vitus*, (St Vitus dance and poisonous bites) *St. Christopher* (travel, storms) *St. Dionisius*, (possession by evil spirits), *St. Ciriacus*, (eye diseases), *St. Acacius*, (diseases of the head), *St. Eustachius*, (burns), *St. Giles*, (lunacy and the evil eye), *St. Margaret*, (kidneys and childbirth), *St. Barbara*, (lightning and sudden death), *St. Catherine* (the study of philosophy).

The feast is celebrated on the first Sunday after the 8th September.

32. St. Leonard – Mosta

This church was built in 1658 by Bernarda
Mangion. *(Acts of the Notary Gian Paolo Fenech of
15th March, 1658).* But Mgr. Dusina reported in 1575
that there existed an earlier church in the same place.

Improvements were effected in 1907 by Dun
Karm Camilleri Chetcuti. He built the belfry, which
has three bells, renovated the interior of the church,
paved it with tiles, installed a pulpit, a Via Crucis, a
lamp and a chandelier, a painted altar front showing
the baptism of St. Leonard, a coat of arms of Pope

Leo XIII and another of the Mangion family. He also commissioned Victor Xerri to paint the ceiling.

The inscription "captivorum salvator" on the main painting is a reminder that St. Leonard of Limoges, a sixth century saint, was considered the protector of slaves. Considering the frequency of Maltese being taken captives by Moslem corsairs from North Africa, it is not surprising that devotion to the saint, probably initiated by the crusaders who stopped at Gozo in 1270, should be strong in these islands. The painting, done in 1640 by Filippo Dingli shows Our Lady of Graces with St. Leonard, St. John the Baptist, St. Bernard and the souls in Purgatory.

The church has one stone altar, a statue of Our Lady of the Rosary donated by Ġammarì Mifsud, one of St. Leonard, the gift of Paċifiku Sammut, and another of St. Anthony given by Dun Karm Dingli.

A bequest by the Mangion family provides for a sung Mass and vespers on the feast day which is held on the first Sunday after the 6th November, when the church is decorated and fireworks are let off.

Various religious groups meet at St. Leonard's.

In the past the Rogation processions on St. Gregory's and St. Mark's days used to go to St. Leonard's, as did the solemn Corpus Christi procession.

33. St. George – Burżebbuġa

This is quite an old church; the first one at Burżebbuġa. After a long period of neglect Bishop Balaguer deconsecrated it in 1659. It was rebuilt in 1682 by the "Roman patrician" Gregorio Bonnici. It had been a juspatronatus, probably granted by the Knights of St. John. One of the descendants of Gregorio, Mgr. Giuseppe Giacomo Testaferrata de Robertis, left a foundation for the celebration of ten Masses and for the lighting of the lamp on Saturdays.

The church is built on a fortified site facing the entrance to the bay of Marsaxlokk. The main door faces seawards, and the back door is on the street behind the church. This back door, up to the last century, had in front of it a drawbridge spanning a ditch which was filled in when the sacristy was built. Above the main door is a damaged coat of arms with the word "Montana" and the date 1628. Clearly it is part of the older church.

During the time when the Order of St. John of Jerusalem ruled over the island, soldiers were posted in this church from which the Order's galleys used to be blessed before sailing on marauding expeditions, mostly aimed at moslem countries.

On Ascension Day, the popular Lapsi feast, the clergy and people of Żurrieq used to proceed to St. George's Bay. After the celebration of Mass at this church the people stayed on to lunch and enjoy themselves by the sea.

After another long period of neglect the church was again opened in 1813 during a bad outbreak of the plague, but was again neglected. It was reopened in 1914 when St. George's Bay began to gain popularity as a summer resort.

A benefactor of St. George's was Chev. Alfred Cachia Zammit who caused it to be paved and furnished with a Via Crucis, a brass chandelier and new vestments. Before the 1939/45 war Mass was celebrated daily and the Rosary recited. Nowadays the only activity consists of the celebration of Mass on Sundays by a member of the Missionary Society of St. Paul.

The titular painting is a copy of the Preti one in St. John's Co-cathedral.

34. Our Lady of
Divine Providence – Siġġiewi

I cannot think of a better description of this graceful church than that given by the poet Father G. Delia, S.J. in his "Tifkiriet". I am unable to translate the music in Fr. Delia's verse, but this is roughly what he says:

"In the silence of these open spaces, among green fields dotted with poppies, under a sky blazing with fire from the rays of the setting sun, you seem to me, dear church of my heart, wrapped in silence and solitude, like a fragment of paradise fallen from the highest heavens in our midst."

Tal-Providenza is situated half-way between Siġġiewi and Għar Lapsi. Long ago there was here the old hamlet of Ħal Kbir, one of the four which gave birth to the present large village of Siġġiewi.

The church was originally dedicated to the Flight to Egypt. While on a pastoral visit, Bishop Alpheran de Bussan deconsecrated it, but during another visit he made on the 28th April, 1747, at the request of the parish priest Dun Mikelanġ Mamo, he reconsecrated it. The people of Siġġiewi went in procession to hear Mass and listen to a panegyric preached by the parish priest. This priest, seeing that cracks had appeared in the walls, demolished the church and built another on the same site. Under the foundation stone, laid by him on the 4th November, 1750, a bronze medal was buried showing Our Lady and the names of Bishop Alpheran and Dun Mikelanġ himself. The latter, as the Bishop's delegate, consecrated the church on the 16th September, 1753. Collections for the building expenses were made by the parish priest aided by Dun Nikol Borg, a saintly man, who paid for the sculpture.

The painting above the only altar, showing Our Lady of Divine Providence, with the Child Jesus, was the work of Enrico Arnaux. Two other paintings of St. Michael and the Souls in Purgatory, are by the same painter. Dun Mikelanġ paid for all of them. Other paintings were done later. In 1804 the main painting was transferred to the sacristy. In its place was hung one by the celebrated Sicilian 18th century painter, Giuseppe Velasco, showing Our Lady blessing the countryside. This painting, and a number of *ex votos*, were stolen in 1984. The Velasco was recovered, but the *ex votos* were not traced.

In 1815-16, Michael Cachia designed the elegant portico and directed its building. It was built to buttress the main building which had been hit by lightning. On the portico ceiling there were stone figures of birds, and below them a Latin inscription of the 26th verse of the VI chapter of the Gospel according to Matthew: "Behold the birds of the air; they do not sow, nor reap, nor store in barns; but your Father who is in heaven looks after them. Are you not worth more than they?"

The church has a pleasing dome and a small belfry with one bell on which appears the coat of arms of Grandmaster Pinto. Devotion to Our Lady of Providence has been strong in the past and many vows and pilgrimages were made and many graces received.

Beside the main altar is a Turkish cannnon-ball of about twelve inches in diameter, reputedly a relic of the Great Siege of 1565 when, among the defenders of Birgu there was a regiment of 560 men of Siġġiewi.

The feast is held on the first or second Sunday in September.

35. Christ the Saviour – Kalkara

This old chapel was severely damaged during the Great Siege of 1565 and had to be demolished by the Knights. After the siege it was rebuilt by Grandmaster La Valette.

Less than a hundred years later it was again rebuilt by the Knight Giovanni Bichi, the architect being the celebrated Lorenzo Gafà. Adjoining it was the palace of the Prior, which from the year 1805 was used by the British Navy as a hospital, known as Ta' Bigi. The new church was blessed by the Vicar General, Canon Famucelli, on the 2nd May, 1651.

Prior Bichi, who was the nephew of Pope Alexander VII, died of the plague on the 24th June, 1676. A marble tablet to his memory was placed in the chapel by his brother, the Cardinal Antonio Bichi. The tablet has been removed but a stone monument with the image of the Prior in bas-relief still exists.

Is-Salvatur is built in the form of a hexagon. Above the door is a statue of the Madonna of the Snows. Inside is one altar which had a painting of St. Philumena by Madiona, now removed.

When Kalkara became a parish its first parish church was the Salvatur chapel. And use was again made of it during the war of 1939/45 when the new parish church was bombed.

Before the war it was very well kept by the people of the neighbourhood. The Services connected with Bigi hospital used to keep it spotlessly clean, the very benches being covered with fine damask.

For some years is-Salvatur was used as a store for the festa decorations. It is now in a bad state.

It is now surrounded by many new buildings. The Cotonera restoration committee is expected to take its renovation in hand shortly.

36. Our Lady of the Visitation
– Żebbuġ

This church is situated in Wied Qirda (Vale of Destruction) which is reached by the road branching left from the Valletta - Siġġiewi motor road, not far from Żebbuġ.

Before the present church was built there was an earlier one dating from the XVI century. Mgr. Dusina visited it on the 2nd February, 1575. It was mentioned by Comm. Abela in 1647. The present church was built by the cleric Bartholomew Magro in 1675. (The number 1678 is scratched on the lintel of the side door). The founder prepared for himself a grave in the church. This can be seen in an inscription on the grave, where he was buried on the 3rd May, 1722, having been murdered by robbers in the farmhouse close to the church.

It is said that before the Knights of St. John came to Malta there used to be a horse patrol stationed by this church, to give early warning to the Mdina garrison of any landing by Barbary corsairs, as well as to protect the neighbouring farmers from robbers.

Although the church is dedicated to the Visit of Our Lady to her cousin St. Elizabeth, it has become to be popularly known as St. Anthony's because there is a statue of the saint in front of which numerous candles and oil lamps used to burn.

The titular painting, said to be the work of Suor Maria de Dominicis, a disciple of Mattia Preti in St. John's Co-Cathedral and who carved the statue of the Immaculate Conception of Bormla, is now kept in the sacristy of Żebbuġ Parish Church. The paintings in this church were stolen some years ago, but have been recovered.

Above the main door, on a ribbon-shaped streamer carved in stone, there is inscribed the first verse of the Magnificat.

37. Our Lady of Graces – Sliema

KILIN

Sliema is not only one of the largest towns of Malta, but also one of the newest. For this reason one does not find in it the old churches one sees in the older villages like Żebbuġ, Rabat, Żejtun, etc. The whole area now covered by Sliema, St. Julian's, Msida and Gzira was until the last century part of the Parish of Birkirkara.

On the rocky promontory now known as Tigné, there was once a small chapel dedicated to Our Lady of Good Voyage. According to tradition, sailors leaving Marsamxett harbour used to salute the Virgin with a Hail Mary, which in Maltese is translated as "Sliema". It is said that the chapel was in fact built in thanksgiving for deliverance from shipwreck.

During the Great Siege of 1565 the "Sliema" promontory was occupied by the besieging Turks and the chapel was practically destroyed. In 1659 it was deconsecrated, but in 1741 a second chapel was built on whose altar hung a painting representing the Madonna, St. Anne, the Child Jesus and St. John the Baptist.

The chapel was very popular with the Knights of St. John, and in 1631 a certain Duminku Seychell left a foundation in its favour. It was well looked after up to the year 1798, when it was destroyed by the occupying French. When the French left and the blockade was finally lifted, it was felt necessary to build another church further inland to serve the growing population of "Tas-Sliema". A certain pious woman, Giovanna Salvaloco, donated a plot of ground on which the chapel of Our Lady of Graces was built in 1803. Here, the first inhabitants used to gather for Sunday Mass. The priest, who used to drive down from Birkirkara knew them all and, after ringing the bell, would not start the services until he was sure that all were present.

The main painting in this church, by an unknown artist, is thought to be the same which used to hang above the altar of the second Tigné chapel. It represents the Holy Family and is a copy of a work by Gianfranco Penni, known as "il Fattore", one of Raphael's pupils. The original is kept at the National Museum of Naples; another copy, signed G.F. is in he "sala delle oche" in the Palazzo dei Conservatori of the Capitoline Museum, while a third copy is in the chapel of France in St. John's Co-cathedral. Of greater artistic value are two large canvases by Mattia Preti, one depicting the Guardian Angel and the other the Holy Family.

The "Tal-Grazzja" church has three small bells, one donated by William Laferla in 1880 and another cast by the Maltese founder Salvu Cauchi in 1834. One of these bells used to sound the knell for felons hanged at "tal-forok" in Floriana, on the opposite side of the harbour; the executions being plainly visible from "Tal-Grazzja" church.

A pink chasuble donated by Grandmaster Pinto which belonged to the "Tal-Grazzja" church is now kept at the parish church of Stella Maris, as is also the iron key of the main door of the second Tigné chapel.

With the rapid increase in the population the need was felt for a bigger church. The Stella Maris church, just in front of "Tal-Grazzja" was built in 1853. That of "Tal-Grazzja" has since then come to be known as "the little church". For some time it continued to be kept open for regular divine service. But at one time the Bishop ordered its closure and the transfer of its belongings to the new church because of a dispute which had cropped up between the lay rector of "Tal-Grazzja" and the Parish Priest.

In the twenties a pious priest, Don Amadeo Bonello, took the chapel in hand and renovated it. He instituted the exposition of the Blessed Eucharist on Sundays, on the first Friday of each month, and during the three Carnival days. Encouraged by his

example a number of persons left legacies to cover
the expenses of these celebrations. The forty hours
Adoration of the Blessed Sacrament, formerly
celebrated at Stella Maris Church is now being held
at "Tal-Grazzja" as is also the one-day adoration of
the Eucharist on the 31st December.

Mass is occasionally celebrated and prayer groups
are held regularly by various organisations. Many
couples choose "Tal-Grazzja" for their wedding
ceremony.

In recent years the ceremony of the Last Supper
of Our Lord has been revived, the Table being
arranged according to old Jewish rites.

The annual festa of "Tal-Grazzja" falls in
mid-September and until a few years ago was
celebrated with due pomp.

A marble slab in the pavement of this church
bears an inscription in memory of two priests, Don
Michele Palma and Dun Tommaso Vassallo, both
former rectors of the Tigné chapel, and a layman,
undoubtedly Michele Pianta, a Maltese knight of St.
John who was a great benefactor of that chapel. These
three personages had been buried in accordance with
their wish at the Tigné chapel and their remains were
translated to the "Tal-Grazzja" church by the Provost
of Birkirkara church in 1856.

DROUGHT AND DISEASE

B esides the constant threat of Moslem attacks the
Maltese were sorely tried by periods of serious
drought, deadly epidemics of the plague and cholera, and
other diseases. A violent earthquake in 1693 caused
widespread destruction. In their distress the Maltese
invoked Our Lady and the saints. (See No. 31).

38. St. Sebastian – Rabat

The church stands at the point where Buskett and College Roads intersect. In the sketch I have included the "Għajn", a combination of horse-trough and village pump, as well as a donkey and cart and a woman wearing the "faldetta". I did so because it is thus that I like to remember the dear and intimate little square opposite San Bastjan where I spent the best years of my boyhood.

This church reminds us of the terrible plague epidemics which periodically ravaged not only Malta but the whole world right up to the nineteenth century. The Maltese used to invoke St. Sebastian and St. Roque for protection from the dread disease. Bishop Molina reports that in this church twelve Masses used to be celebrated on the feast-day of the saint and two more on St. Roque's day. Mgr. Dusina mentions the vow made during the 1519 epidemic to satisfy which, since that year until a few years ago, the Canons of the Cathedral and the friars of the various convents of Rabat used to go in procession from the Cathedral to St. Sebastian's on the 20th January. I recall vividly how, as a little boy in the twenties, I used to be impressed by the sight of the solemn-faced mace-bearer, in white wig and red and purple robes, shouldering the heavy gilt mace, marching at the head of the Chapter.

St. Sebastian's is quite old. By a will dated 13th September, 1471, in the acts of Notary Luqa Sillato, Edward Zammit left ten florins for the building of a room for the sacristan. (According to Achille Ferres it was Orlando Zabbar who left the money, and the will is dated 13th September, 1477). Ludovico Galea renovated the church, and on the 27th December, 1732 Bishop Alpheran de Bussan blessed it. Then, in 1782 the field beside it was leased to Diegu Cuschieri.

This is a lovely church, both inside and on the outside. The titular painting shows the martyrdom of St. Sebastian. This is flanked by paintings of Pope St. Gregory the Great and St. Roque. The latter was transferred from a church dedicated to Our Lady which existed at the entrance to Mdina, called Madonna della Porta. Paintings on either side of the aisle show Our Lady of Graces, St. Paul, St. Joseph and St. Louis, king of France. Four small round paintings in the dome represent the four Evangelists.

The church is lovingly looked after by the Sisters of Charity who, some fifty years ago moved to the house next to it where they ran a kindergarten. Their former house and school was in St. Dominic's Square. That was the first school I attended. Unfortunately the nuns have now closed their school.

St. Sebastian's now has a "table" altar and decent benches, and is paved with tiles. Mass is celebrated daily by the priests of the Missionary Society of St. Paul. Spiritual retreats are occasionally held, and on Sundays the M.U.S.E.U.M. Society hold conferences. During October the Rosary is recited daily. On the Saint's day first vespers are sung and a High Mass celebrated.

39. St. Anthony the Abbot
– Xagħra, Gozo

This is one of the oldest churches in Gozo, reported to have been in existence in 1400. According to old documents it was built by the gozitan family of Camire and Hinzi. This is confirmed by the report of Mgr. Dusina (1575). In 1601 the chapel was rebuilt with a cemetery, or "zuntier" in front of it.

It became the first parish church of Xagħra on the 28th April, 1688, when Xagħra and three other new parishes were created by Bishop Cocco Palmeri.

The Blessed Sacrament was kept in it for the first time on 5th June, 1688. The first Parish Priest was Dun Bernard Formosa. The church served as parish church until 1692.

The plague of 1814, which carried off 104 victims, was fiercest in the area around the church. The first three victims were buried in its cemetery. They were Anġlu Galea, his daughter Rużarja, and Kasimiru Rapa. When the plague passed, certain articles which were in the church, including the old painting, were burnt in order to disinfect the place. The damask covering the walls was taken down to Ramla Bay and steeped in sea water for forty days, at the end of which time it was quite useless. The present painting, depicting St. Anthony with the people of Xaghra living under tents during the plague, was painted by Dun Salv Bondì in 1816. When the church was renovated in 1847 the organ gallery was built.

The church was hit during the war of 1939-45. It was accordingly condemned by Bishop Michael Gonzi. But his successor, Mgr. Giuseppe Pace, noted for his devotion to St. Anthony, took early steps to have the church repaired. He nominated for this task Dun Ġużepp Farrugia. When the latter died, the work was entrusted to Dun Samwel Formosa. In September, 1947, the Bishop reconsecrated the church. It was later enlarged when the zuntier was built upon. It was blessed anew by Bishop Pace on 13th November, 1955. A new statue was made of St. Anthony surrounded by animals which symbolize his temptations. It is by Wistin Camilleri.

The church was consecrated by Bishop Nicholas Cauchi on the 28th April, 1988. A new belfry was built and a new statue of St. Anthony the Abbot, by Michael Camilleri Cauchi, was blessed by the Bishop on 17th January, 1988. Unfortunately the well intentioned renovation has done away with the original character of the church.

Since 1948 the feast of the saint, which falls on the 17th January, has included the ceremony of the blessing of animals. The tiny square in front of the church is on that day well decorated, and a throne is set up for the Bishop. In the morning the Bishop says Mass and delivers a speech. Then he blesses a number of rusks and a quantity of oats.

These rusks and oats commemorate an ancient practice when, in fulfilment of an obligation, during vespers and on the eve of the feast, a measure of wheat made into bread and a jar of wine were distributed to the poor.

In the evening the Bishop walks in procession from the Collegiate Church of Xagħra to St. Anthony's accompanied by the Chapter and the clergy. Arrived in front of the church he blesses the animals. These are usually cattle, horses, donkeys, dogs, rabbits, kittens, guinea-pigs and birds. After the blessing the owners leading their beasts file past the Bishop. To each of them he gives a picture of the Saint, a bag of oats, and a rusk.

This is always an attractive ceremony because the owners of the animals vie with each other in decorating their pets with many-coloured ribbons and other ornaments. People from all the island flock to Xagħra for this festa, the like of which is not to be seen anywhere else in Gozo. After the ceremony the Xagħra band plays marches all the way to the main square.

The Blessed Sacrament is kept permanently in St. Anthony's, Mass is celebrated daily, and in the evening the Rosary is recited and Benediction imparted.

40. Our Lady of Sorrows
– Tal-Pietà

KILIN

S hortly after the building of the city of Valletta there was an outbreak of the plague. The victims were buried outside the outer fortifications. Close to the newly-formed cemetery a small chapel dedicated to St. Roque was built in 1590. Adjacent to it the Augustinian fathers built a convent in 1617. The chapel, built practically on the sea-shore, came to be known as "Santa Maria a mare", or Tal-Pietà.

In 1652 Pope Innocent X ordered the closure of all convents having only a small community. The Augustinians had to leave.

In 1714, as the population around the chapel had grown to 456, and as to hear Mass these people had to go to the Parish Church of St. Paul in Valletta, Bishop Gori Mancini made the "Duluri" chapel a sub-parish. But when in 1740 the parish church of St. Publius of Floriana was built, the Tal-Pietà chapel lost that privilege.

"Id-Duluri" then fell on bad times and was in danger of collapsing. Cleric Giuseppe Spiteri proposed to rebuild it on condition that it become a lay benefice. Bishop Alpheran gave his assent on the 12th October, 1757.

The Knight Fra Wolfgang Philip Von Guttenberg, in fulfilment of a vow made during a plague epidemic, donated a large bas-relief on wood of St. John the Baptist bearing the inscription "Praemium veritatis", and below this the head of the Saint on a platter.

In the middle of the church are the graves of two Knights, Fra Guillaume de Bernart d'Avernes, and Fra Vincenzo Ruffo, who died of the plague in 1676.

The patriot Dun Gejtan Mannarino and his fellow plotters used to meet at this church to prepare the "Revolt of the Priests" against the Order of St. John of Jerusalem.

The "Duluri" church has four side chapels, a sacristy, the old convent, and a garden.

The titular painting is of Our Lady of Sorrows and is ornamented with baroque sculpture. In one of the side chapels is a painting of Our Lady of Loreto, with St. John the Baptist and Blessed Gerard (founder of the Order of St John of Jerusalem) and the coat of arms and portrait of the person who paid for it. In the St. Roque chapel is a painting of St. Joseph by Carlo Gimach. In another chapel the painting is of Our Lady of Graces, with St. John, St. Ambrose, St. Nicholas of Tolentino, with the date 1624, and some ex votos. In the fourth chapel is a large crucifix. The statue of Our Lady of Sorrows was the gift of Bishop Alpheran. There is also a more recent statue of Our Lady of Sorrows and another of St. Joseph.

The Duluri chapel was originally in the parish of Valetta, but passed to that of Floriana (1844), Msida (1867) and later Fatima. Mass is celebrated daily.

41. St. Roque – Balzan

T his church, built in 1593 during an outbreak of
the plague, is situated in a tiny square called "the
square of the three churches." The other two
churches are The Annunciation, which was the first
parish church of the village, and St. Leonard's, now
converted into a dwelling house.

St. Roque's had a cemetery beside it, and in front
of it is the characteristic village cross.

The church is well kept, but no religious services
are held in it.

42. St. Roque – Valletta

KILIN

St. Roque's was built in fulfilment of a vow made by the Jurats of the Università dei Grani, during the plague of 1593. *(Acts of Notary Ascanio Scaglia of the 24th March, 1593)*. The Confraternity of St. Roque, now extinct, was formed at the same time. To commemorate their deliverance the Jurats instituted the yearly horse and donkey race, still run on St. Roque's feast day. On the same day the clergy of the Parish church of St. Paul of Valletta used in the past to hold a votive procession.

When plague broke out again in 1675-76, the
Jurats obtained the Bishop's sanction for the
enlargment of the church. Work started in 1680 under
the supervision of the architect Lorenzo Gafà.
Grandmaster Gregorio Carafa made a handsome
contribution towards the expenses, a fact
commemorated in an inscription above the church
door. Vicar General Ludovico Famucelli, who was
also Assessor and Pro-Inquisitor, blessed the church
on 12th August, 1681.

The Jesus and Mary Sodality was formed in the
year 1641. Its members used to meet and pray every
day, and during Carnival they made penance,
organised a forty-hour adoration of the Blessed
Sacrament, and joined in an Eucharistic procession
led by the clergy of St. Paul's, of which parish the
church of St. Roque forms part. The Sodality is still
active.

St. Roque's is the home of the Institution of
Christian Doctrine, formed in 1864 by the cleric Dr.
Francesco Spiteri Agius, who founded similar
institutions for boys and girls at the churches of St.
James, Our Lady of Victories, Our Lady of the Pilar,
St. Barbara, and the Jesuits' church in Valletta, besides
other institutions in Tarxien. The St. Roque institution
was placed under the protection of Our Lady of
Graces and the Saints Catherine and Agatha. It is
still very much alive. The meetings, which used to
be held in a corridor adjacent to the sacristy, were
later held in rooms opposite St. Roque's. The titular
painting of the institution is by Gagliardi.

The main painting at St. Roque's, which shows
the Immaculate Conception with St. Roque, St.

Angelo the Martyr, and the victims of the plague, is by Stefano Erardi. Also by Erardi is a painting of St. Stephen above one of the side altars. The painting opposite is by Palombi. There is another small painting of St. Paul of the Cross, founder of the Passionist Fathers. A Confraternity of St. Paul of the Cross was formed in 1932.

The main altar is partly in marble. The beaten silver and gilt monstrance is a gift of the Jesus and Mary Sodality. One of the two silver lamps was donated by the Sodality, the other being a gift of Grandmaster Pinto. The organ is of the sixteenth century. It is still in very good condition.

The church has recently been extensively renovated. Mass is celebrated on Saturdays and Sundays.

43. St. Roque
– Birkirkara

This church, situated not far from the Basilica of St. Helen, was built after the plague of 1592 in fulfilment of a vow made by the villagers to St. Roque. It had a vaulted roof and a zuntier. A Żebbuġ lady endowed it with a benefice of two scudi a year.

Finding it neglected, Bishop Balaguer Camarasa deconsecrated it on 23rd March, 1659. But shortly afterwards, on the 18th March, 1676, while another plague epidemic was raging, Canon Martin Cauchi together with Peter Gatt, James Pullicino, Matthew

Grech and Mario Gatt petitioned the bishop for its reopening. Besides the expenses needed to repair it, these five offered a yearly benefice of eighty-six scudi. The request was granted. It is recounted that the people who lived in the quarter behind this church were not touched by the plague which killed 11,300 people, mostly in Birkirkara.

With the passing of time the church was again neglected. In 1863 it was rebuilt, thanks to the efforts of Dun Philip Grech. The Provost of Birkirkara, Dr. Kalċidon Agius, acting as the Bishop's delegate, solemnly blessed it on the 9th August, 1863. Since then it has seen other bad times. Today it is well kept. In June 1964 Paul Micallef donated a statue of St. Rita and a festa was held to mark the occasion, Monsignor Galea presiding. The feast of St. Rita has been celebrated every year since then.

The graceful little belfry has five bells. Outside, on the left of the church is a statue of St. Roque. The church has one altar with the main painting showing Our Lady of Graces flanked by St. Roque and St. Sebastian. There is also an organ and a statue of St. Roque.

The feast is celebrated in August, and Mass is said daily.

44. Saint Lucy – Għaxaq

This church lies on the Tarxien - Gudja Road. The new residential area of Santa Luċija took its name from it.

It was built in 1535 on land belonging to the Cathedral. It was a canonical church providing a prebend for one of the Cathedral canons who, in turn, was obliged to bear the expenses of the feast and to distribute a sum of money to the poor on the feast-day. The custom existed up to the second world war.

The church was rebuilt by Paolo Pellegrino, and the sacristy annexed to it by Wiġi Agius.

There is one altar the main painting on which, showing Our Lady with the Child Jesus and a kneeling St. Lucy, has been removed.

In a corner of the zuntier is a well which used to provide drinking water to thirsty pilgrims.

The festa used to be celebrated on the 13th December, with the singing of vespers and a High Mass, the Ghaxaq clergy concelebrating Mass on the feast day. This has been discontinued and the church is neglected.

THE KNIGHTS

A mong the many noble buildings left by the Knights Hospitallers of St. John of Jerusalem, who ruled over Malta from 1530 to 1798, are several churches, chief among them the Co-Cathedral of St. John in Valletta. The various Langues had their own churches (Italy - St. Catherine's; Aragón - Our Lady of Pilar; Castille - St. James) In addition individual knights built some of the smaller churches.

45. St. Anthony the Abbot
– Buskett, Rabat

This church forms part of the Verdala Palace complex. Building started under Grandmaster Raphael Cotoner and was completed on his death in 1664 by his brother, Grandmaster Nicholas Cotoner.

The marvellous paintings behind the altar and at the sides are by Mattia Preti. The main one shows the Madonna with the child Jesus, with St. John the Baptist and St. Anthony the Abbot kneeling at her feet. Some years ago this painting was sent to Naples and placed on show with other works of the famous painter. It is in excellent condition. The smaller paintings on the sides depict St. Nicholas of Bari and the Archangel Raphael, the patron saints of the Cotoner brothers. Other paintings by Preti's pupils are of Christ appearing to St. Thomas, and the beheading of St. John the Baptist.

In a niche by the main altar is a statue of St. Rita, made in 1957 by Wistin Camilleri. It enjoys such devotion that the chapel has come to be known as the chapel of St. Rita, and her feast, which falls on the Sunday nearest to the 22nd of May, is very popular.

The church has been in the hands of the Augustinians since 1944. They are rendering an invaluable pastoral service among the farmers of the Buskett area. For a time the Legion of Mary used to hold their meetings in the church, where catechism has been taught for many years.

Since some twenty-two years heads of State and other important visitors to Malta have been received at Verdala Palace. For reasons of security the chapel of St. Anthony was kept closed for ten years. In 1996, at the instance of Dr. Daniel Micallef, then Speaker of the House of Representatives, and the rector, Fr. Raphael Azzopardi, the church was reopened to the public. The Archpriest of Rabat, Dun Benjamin Tonna, blessed it and celebrated Mass attended by a very large crowd.

46. The Immaculate Conception
Wied Gerżuma – Rabat

G randmaster Antoine de Paule (1621-36) bought some land in Malta and Gozo and devoted the rent collected from the leases to the building of galleys for the Order. One of the areas was Wied Gerżuma, which overlooks Fomm-ir-riħ bay and is one of the most pleasant spots in the Rabat hinterland. To reach the church, drive past the Roman Villa on the way to Fiddien. At Fiddien bridge turn right and follow the signs to Kunċizzjoni.

In the year 1736, Grandmaster Antonio Manuel de Vilhena built this chapel. The arched gateway beside the zuntier bears the inscription: "Fondazione Paola, 1736" and the coat of arms of De Paule.

One of the most attractive rural feasts is held annually here. It dates back from the time of the Knights, who used to travel from Rabat on horseback.

When Napoleon Bonaparte ousted the Knights of St. John, the property of the Order became Government property. The Immaculate Conception is one of the churches which are still owned by the State.

The church has one altar with a beautiful painting of the Virgin and Child, St. Joseph, St. John the Baptist, St. Paul and St. Anthony of Padua. It is by Gian Nicola Buhagiar. Attributed to the same artist are two small paintings of St. Joachim and St. Anne, which flank the altarpiece. There is also a statue of the Immaculate Conception. On the left of the zuntier is a well.

Figures of old ships are scratched on the façade. These were probably done to satisfy vows made by sailors saved from drowning. Others like them are to be seen at the Conception church of Qala, Gozo.

The festa is held on the first Sunday after the 8th December.

Mass is celebrated on Sundays, and spiritual retreats are often held in this church.

47. St. Julian - Senglea

KILIN

The city of Senglea takes its name from Claude
de la Sengle, Grandmaster of the Order of St.
John from 1553 to 1557, who founded it in 1554.

Long before the Order came to Malta in 1530 the
peninsula on which Senglea is built was an
uninhabited hill on which stood the original chapel
built around the beginning of the fourteenth century.
The Knights, who loved the chase, named the chapel
after St. Julian, patron saint of hunters. They lost no
time in fortifying Birgu and erecting fort St. Michael

on St. Julian's hill. In the year 1539, the Portuguese Knight Fra Diego Pires de Malfreire rebuilt the chapel of St. Julian.

Soon after the terrible trial of the Great Siege (1565) the population of Senglea increased rapidly, but laboured under the disadvantage of having to cross over to Birgu for their spiritual needs. In 1575 the Sengleans petitioned the Apostolic Visitor, Mgr. Dusina, to assign a priest to St. Julian's. The request was acceded to, on condition that Senglea continue to form part of the parish of Birgu, and that baptisms had to be administered at St. Lawrence's in Birgu. Don Erasmus was the first vice parish-priest at St. Julian's.

Five years later building started on the much bigger church dedicated to the Birth of Our Lady, which became the parish church of Senglea in 1581, Don Antonio de Nicolaci being the first parish priest. In 1588 a small school for children was opened at St. Julian's by Father Vincent Caruana. This was one of the very first schools in Malta. Up to the year 1592 there was a cemetery near the church. In 1612 the Congregation of the Onorati was formed at St. Julian's, but later transferred to the parish church.

In 1624 Bishop Cagliares placed St. Julian's under the care of the Augustinian Discalced Friars, but these stayed only one year. Bishop Alpheran de Bussan later declared St. Julian the special patron saint of Senglea, together with Our Lady and St. Philip Neri.

Towards the year 1660 St. Julian's was in a very bad state. It was pulled down in 1699 and rebuilt under architect Lorenzo Gafà, the work being completed in 1712. The altar-piece was painted in 1699 by Raimondo de Domenico.

Mass is celebrated daily, prayer groups meet at St. Julian's, and the feast of the Saint is celebrated on the 27th January.

48. Our Lady of Loreto – Gudja

This graceful church was in danger of being demolished when the new runway of Luqa airport was bein planned. It is situated just across the road bordering the runway.

It was built in 1548 by the Knight Imbert de Morines as an act of thanksgiving after the battle with a Turkish force which took place in the vicinity. Two high mounds of stones nearby are said to cover the corpses of those of the enemy who died in the encounter. In the sacristy there is a painting on wood, by an unknown artist, depicting the Knight kneeling before the Virgin and Child who appear above the House of Loreto borne aloft by angels. An inscription reads: 'Fra Imbert de Murines, Priore de Alvernia MDXXXXVIII." The arched top of the panel is divided into three sections containing a central Crucifixion group flanked on one side by the kneeling Virgin and, on the other by the Announcing Angel.

Soon after the erection of the church many Knights and Maltese pilgrims began to visit it on Saturday afternoons. To shelter these pilgrims, procurator Luke Vella built two loggias which one can still see beside the church. A plaque bears the name of Vella and the date, 2nd July, 1550. In a room nearby a parchment was discovered vouching for the devotion of the visiting Knights.

The plague of 1676 carried off over 11,000 of the 61,000 inhabitants of the island. The survivors enlarged the sanctuary, through public contributions organised by Archpriest Dun Viċenz Grixti.

Dun Ġwann Bonnici restored the church in 1820. And in 1837 Pope Gregory XVI granted various indulgences. Dun Salv Formosa paved the church with mosaic and planted the olive trees that surround it.

The fine titular painting shows the Virgin above the clouds surrounded by angels, with St. John the Baptist and a female saint (St. Rita or St. Margaret) below her.

A delicate statuette of the Virgin and Child, carved out of Gozitan marble, donated by Captain de Werberg in 1535 was mislaid, but later recovered from the bottom of a well.

In the sacristy is a ceramic plate with the coat of arms of Bishop Gargallo (1578-1614). Another curious object is a very large eggshell.

During the 1939/45 war the church was occupied by the Army. A bomb hit did very little damage. The church was deconsecrated, but soon after the end of the war it was reconsecrated, restored, and solemnly blessed by Dun Anton Rapa, Parish Priest of Gudja, as the delegate of Bishop coadjutor Michael Gonzi. By a curious coincidence during the blessing a large number of planes landed close by. President Roosevelt had arrived in Malta, on his way to the Yalta summit.

Members of the Żammit family took good care of the church for two hundred years. Included in their number were Dun Feliċ Zammit (1867), Parish Priest of Gudja; Dun Karm and Dun Luret Zammit and, up to 1960 by Antonio Zammit. Another member of the family sent a gift of brass candlesticks from Australia!

I remember Manwel Azzopardi who looked after the Bir Miftuħ church as well, keeping this church immaculately clean.

The feast is celebrated on the first Sunday in December.

49. Our Lady Ta' Liesse – Valletta

KILIN

This church, situated not far from the Custom House, has enjoyed great veneration by the people of the port area.

It was built in 1620 by Fra Giacomo De Chess du Bellay, Bailiff of Armenia. The ceremony of the laying of the first stone, which took place on the 21st November of that year, was attended by the Grand Master, Alof de Wignacourt, the Grand Prior Urrea de Camarasa, and many of the Knights of the order, including the founder. The church belonged to the

Langue of France and took the name of Our Lady venerated at the sanctuary of Liesse, near Laon, in Picardy.

With the name there goes a story, according to which, in the year 1134, three young noblemen, the Seigneur d'Eppe, the Seigneur de Marçois and their younger brother, were captured by the Saracens at the siege of Askalon, and carried off to Egypt.

The Sultan tried to convert them to the Moslem faith. When he saw that all his efforts were of no avail, he sent his daughter Ismeria who was very well versed in that religion. But instead of converting them it was they who converted her. She loved to hear about the Blessed Virgin, and one day she promised to become a Christian if they made her a statue of Our Lady. She provided tools and material, but the youths unfortunately were no artists. That night, a blinding light shone in the prison, sweet singing was heard, and the three young men saw a beautiful statue of the Virgin. Helped by Ismeria they fled and walked away until they fell down completely exhausted. They fell asleep, and on waking found themselves in Picardy. There they built the church of Liesse (which means happiness). Ismeria changed her name to Mary.

This story referred to by Bosio, is commemorated in the main painting at Ta' Liesse, done by Enrico Arnaux, and in other canvases now hanging in the corridor of the convent of the Minor Franciscans in Valletta, as well as embroidered on four red capes, given by Grand Master Jean Paul de Lascaris, now kept in the museum of the Co-cathedral of St. John.

Very similar to the Ismeria story is the 'Captive's Tale' in chapters 39 and 41 of the first part of Don Quijote, in which Cervantes gives a vivid description of action in the Battle of Lepanto, where he himself was wounded.

The Ta' Liesse church was rebuilt in 1740 by the Langue of France, and blessed by Monsignor Rull, Grand Prior of the Order. It was solemnly consecrated by Bishop Labini on the 23rd November, 1806. This is commemorated by a marble plaque.

A large number of *ex votos*, left by various people, including French Knights, have now been removed. Fra Giuseppe Artau paid for a marble main altar, brought from St. Elmo a statue of the Virgin, and from Fort Manuel transferred the body of St. Generoso, martyr, which was placed under the altar of St. Louis, King of France.

Besides the said two altars there is another dedicated to St. Maurus, Abbot. The cupola is graceful and so is the belfry designed by Francesco Zammit.

With the departure of the Knights of St. John, the church of Ta' Liesse became Government property. It was hit by German bombs during the last war, but repaired. On the 27th September, 1961, Government, in agreement with the Bishop, gave the church to the Apostolate of the Sea.

The church is kept open every day up to noon, and Mass is celebrated at 6.45 a.m. On Sundays two Masses are celebrated, at 7.15 and 9.30. The feast is held on the first Sunday in July, with a triduum in which the story of the three captives is recounted.

50. The Lourdes Chapel – Floriana

The Capuchin Friars look after this chapel built in the square in front of their Floriana convent.

An older chapel existed in the same place. It was dedicated to St. Mary Magdalen and had been built in 1709 by the Knight Fra Wolfgang Von Guttenberg, Bailiff of Brandenburg.

In 1881 Father Provincial Philip Anton from Valletta replaced the statue of the Magdalen by one of Our Lady of Lourdes. The reclining stone Magdalen, which had been taken to the convent was destroyed during a Nazi air-raid.

The present chapel was built by Fr. Francis helped by Francis Xavier Galea on a design by Chev. Emmanuel Borg. Work began in July, 1918, the builder being Piju Ebejer. Dominic Busuttil constructed a "cave" similar to the one at Lourdes. The marble sculpture was done by Joseph Sammut and Salvu Buhagiar. The dome, which covers the chapel rests on columns.

On the 26th December. 1920, Archbishop Dom Maurus Caruana blessed the chapel. On the same day the statue of the Madonna was placed inside the artificial cave. On the 9th February, 1923, the altar was consecrated by the same Archbishop.

Several benefactors have contributed towards the decoration. Among them were Sir Michelangelo Refalo who paid for the marble pavement; Marquis Scicluna who donated the silver aureola, and Francis Xavier Galea who carried out many other works. The names of the benefactors are inscribed on a marble slab on the façade.

Besides those of Our Lady and St. Bernadette there are statues of the Blessed Heart of Jesus and of St. Joseph.

Before the last war, instead of the cross, there was on top of the dome a stone angel with wings outstretched. When the capuchins' church and convent were hit during the war, the friars used the Lourdes chapel to carry on with their pastoral work.

The Lourdes chapel is today a centre of Marian devotions. Commemorations of the Lourdes apparitions take place in February, March, April and July.

51. Our Lady of Miracles – Lija

Situated at the geographical centre of Malta, this church can be reached either from Attard, bypassing St. Catherine's hospital on the road to Mosta, or from Lija.

Long ago there existed on this spot another church dedicated to the Assumption, probably the principal one of Hal Bordi. That village was joined to Attard when the latter became a parish in 1575, but later became part of Lija when it became a parish in 1609. Close to this old church there was a cemetery.

The present church was built by Grandmaster Nicholas Cotoner in 1664, the architect probably being Lorenzo Gafà. The principal painting is by Mattia Preti, and shows Our Lady and the Child Jesus flanked by St. Peter, St. Nicholas and the Archangel Raphael, the last two being the patron saints of the Cotoner brothers, both Grandmasters of the Order. The Madonna is known as Tas-Silġ, (of the snows) although the church is dedicated to the Assumption.

Since the sixteenth century great devotion has been shown to a triptych of the Madonna which can be seen in a niche on the right of the altar. This painting is the only thing left of the old church. Devotion to this image grew as never before when one day tears were seen to flow from the eyes of the Madonna. On the day when this happened there occurred a violent earthquake, probably that of the 21st February, 1743.

Bishop Alpheran de Bussan, during a visit he made in 1747 described the picture in these words: "the Madonna, known as The Miraculous, painted on wood covered with glass and having a sculptured frame, is held in great veneration."

The church was consecrated by Bishop Labini on 23rd December, 1787, when relics of St. Peter, St. Catherine, St. Calcedonius, St. Teopista and St. Columbanus were placed inside the altar. In 1840 the body of St. Mansueta, Virgin and Martyr, was brought from Rome and placed in a niche on the left of the altar, opposite the miraculous Madonna.

When revolution broke out in Rome in 1848, Cardinal Gabriel Ferretti, cousin of Pope Pio Nono, came to Malta and stayed with the Delicata family near this church. He used to say Mass every day in the church. Before leaving Malta he left a bouquet of artificial flowers made of seashells. A tablet in the sacristy commemorates the visit.

During the war of 1939/45 the miraculous picture was taken to Lija parish church for safe keeping. It is now back at Tal-Mirakli. Among the votive offerings is a silver lamp donated by Grandmaster De Vilhena, an artistic crucifix carved in wood, a silver censer, a set of candlesticks, and many paintings. Two of the paintings, both by Lazzaro Mallia, are of St. Michael and of St. Philip. They were done in 1794.

The organ gallery was built in 1829.

Many buildings have gone up around the church during the past twenty years and Tal-Mirakli has become a centre of pastoral activity. The festa is celebrated on the last Sunday in May.

52. Ta' Sarria – Floriana

S oon after the building of Valletta, the Knight Fra
Martin de Sarria Navarro bought a piece of land
outside the city and on it built the first Sarria church.
This was in 1585 during the Grandmastership of
Verdalle.

Ta' Sarria was the first church built in Floriana
and served the religious needs of seamen. This can
be seen from the first titular painting, now kept in
the National Museum. It was painted on wood by
Antonio Riccio of Messina, and shows Our Lady, St.

John the Baptist and St. Lucy. Below these appear galleys of the Order and the kneeling figures of De Sarria and Grandmaster Verdalle. The painting is known as "the Madonna of the Galleys".

The connection with seamen was a long-standing one. In 1791, the Venetian admiral Angelo Emo stopped at Malta to repair the damage suffered in an attack on Tunis, and wintered here. He fell sick and died on the 1st March 1792 and was buried in the Sarria church after a solemn funeral.

Several knights administered the church, took good care of it, and effected repairs. Among them were Fra Giovanni Morizzi, Fra Luca Bueno, who later became Bishop of Malta and Fra Saverio Muscat.

In the year 1675 a virulent plague epidemic left over eight thousand victims. Grandmaster Nicholas Cotoner made a vow to rebuild the Sarria church, a vow confirmed by a decree of the Council on 11th April 1676. The first stone was laid on the 6th December, 1676. The architect was probably Mattia Preti. The lantern built atop the dome proved too heavy and was replaced by an eight-pointed cross.

Many of the paintings in Sarria are by Mattia Preti. His are the St. Michael and St. John, in the lunettes, which were restored in 1952, as well as the paintings of the saints to whom the Maltese used to pray during plague epidemics, namely: Roque, Sebastian, Rosalia and Nicholas of Bari. Also by Preti is the titular showing the Immaculate Conception, treading on the head of Satan, with the victims of the plague looking up to her while two angels, one sheathing his sword and another breaking it, symbolise the end of the calamity.

On the 21st September, 1724, seeing that the suburb of Floriana was growing rapidly, Grandmaster De Vilhena petitioned the Pope for the designation of Sarria church as parish church. But as Sarria was administered by the Chaplains of the Order and was not subject to the Bishop, the latter (Gori Mancini), objected suggesting that another church be built.

The Grandmaster agreed, and the first stone of the church of St. Publius was laid on the 2nd August, 1733, by Bishop Alpheran de Bussan.

The Napoleonic troops did not fail to leave their mark at Ta' Sarria, by defacing the coats of arms of the Order and of Cotoner which appeared on the door.

On the 6th December 1924 the Jesuits took over the administration of Ta' Sarria. Among their activities, besides the daily celebration of Masses, are the holding of retreats and spiritual exercises, the institution of the Apostleship of Prayer, the publication of the Messenger of the Sacred Heart, the Crusader, and other books.

At Ta' Sarria the saintly Dun Gorg Preca used to assemble the members of the M.U.S.E.U.M. Society, of which he was the founder, once a week.

During the war, after the Church of St. Publius was hit by German bombs on the 28th April, 1942, the Sarria church served as parish church up to the 10th December, 1944. This is commemorated in a plaque placed in the Sarria sacristy by the Floriana Civic Committee.

The church is round in form, has one altar, and three bells. One of the bells, bearing the image of the Immaculate Conception, was blessed in 1824. The smaller ones, bearing images of St. John and St. Joseph were blessed in 1888.

Besides the Preti paintings there is one of St. Anne, by Falzon, and another of St. Benedict Joseph Labre, by P. Darmanin. In the sacristy are paintings of Fra De Sarria and Grandmaster Cotoner. There are statues of the Sacred Heart of Jesus, the Ecce Homo, Our Lady of Sorrows, the Immaculate Conception, and the Jesuit saints Luigi Gonzaga and Francis Xavier.

On the feast of the Immaculate Conception a votive procession from St. John's in Valletta goes to Ta' Sarria.

THE FRENCH OCCUPATION

The Knights of St. John surrendered these islands to Napoleon Bonaparte when he touched at Malta on his way to Egypt. Shortly afterwards the Maltese revolted and, with the help of Portugal and the Kingdom of Naples, as well as that of the blockading British Navy, forced the French to withdraw.

The French left their mark on the churches when in various chapels they slashed paintings of Our Lady.

53. The Immaculate Conception
– St. Julian's

When the Prior of Lombardy, the Bailiff Fra Paolo Raffaele Spinola built for himself the fine palace overlooking the picturesque bay which bears his name, he built close to it the church of the Immaculate Conception. The first stone was laid on the 16th June, 1687, and the church was blessed by Grand Prior Fra Pierre Viany on the 10th September, 1688.

The façade was enlarged in 1914 when Fr. Angelo Portelli O.P. was auxiliary Bishop.

The titular painting is by an unknown artist. There are paintings of Our Lady of the Rosary by Giuseppe Arena and of St. Expeditus, martyr, and portraits of Bailiff Spinola and Bishop Angelo Portelli.

The Maltese patriot Dun Gejtan Mannarino, who had been imprisoned in fort St. Elmo for his part in the abortive "rebellion of the priests" of the 8th September, 1775, and who was set free by Napoleon Bonaparte, came to end his days, in great poverty, in a small room adjacent to this church.

Mass is celebrated daily.

54. St. Anne - Pwales, St. Paul's Bay

This church can be seen built on the rocky hillside to the right of the St. Paul's Bay - Għajn Tuffieħa road.

An older church built on the same site was dedicated to the Nativity of Our Lady. The present church was built by Dun Gio Vincenzo Galea. It was deconsecrated, but subsequently reconsecrated by Bishop Astiria on the 1st July, 1672.

The occupying French soldiers of Napoleon, who slaughtered cattle in the vicinity, wreaked considerable damage to the church, firing their muskets at the door and windows, and slashing the picture of Our Lady with their bayonets.

A new painting by Dun Ġużepp de Stefano, done in 1860, represents St. Anne, St. Joachim and the young Virgin Mary.

The church, which is a juspatronatus of Count Sant Fournier, was renovated some sixty years ago, when the walls were buttressed, the floor paved, and electricity installed.

Besides the titular painting there are those of the Sacred Heart of Jesus, Our Lady of Sorrows and St. Joseph, a Via Crucis, and statues of the Immaculate Conception and of St. Anthony of Padua.

The bell-cot, furnished with a new bell, was rebuilt in 1966.

The chapel is mentioned in Ninu Cremona's dramatic poem "il-fidwa tal-bdiewa".

Spiritual retreats are occasionally held here.

55. St. Joseph – Manikata

Not far from St. Anne's is this church which served the spiritual needs of the hamlet of Manikata until the new, modern-style church, one of the masterpieces of architect Richard England was built. It is not very old, and has one altar with a painting by Ramiro Calì. This painting is now in the new Manikata church.

56. San Ġwann tal-Għargħar
– San Ġwann

KILIN

This old church was deconsecrated by Bishop Balaguer on the 23rd March, 1659. Up to that year burials used to take place in the zuntier. It was rebuilt in 1672 by Peter Gatt who paid for the celebration of the feast of the beheading of St. John the Baptist, and for lighting the lamp on Saturdays. But up to the year 1680, when Bishop Molina visited it, it still had not been reconsecrated. Molina ordered that with moneys collected at St. John's, vespers were to be sung on the eve of the feast, and Mass celebrated on St. John's day at the parish church of St. Helena in Birkirkara.

It was close to this little church that the leader of the Birkirkara insurgents, Borg "Braret" was the first to raise the British flag on the battery commanded by him which was bombarding the French besieged inside Valletta.

No religious functions are today held in St. John's.

Something unusual in this chapel is the eight-pointed cross surmounting the bell-cot. Note also the star-shaped air vent on the room next to it. The painting of the beheading of St. John is said to be very old.

57. St. Peter – Qormi

Below the graceful bell-cot of this church is a statue of St. Peter surmounting the coat of arms of Bishop Balaguer Camarasa. At the two corners are cannon-shaped water spouts. The church has one altar with the titular painting of St. Peter's martyrdom.

The church was built in the 16th century. In 1656 Bishop Balaguer deconsecrated it. It was rebuilt by Dun Peter Cassia whose house stood beside it. This priest bequeathed his house to the church (*Acts of*

Not. Borg Pace), and cleric Ġużepp Grech left moneys for the lighting of the lamp on the saint's day. And in the acts of Notary Luċju Azzopardi, of the 2nd February, 1656, the sisters Paska and Minka Axisa left 100 scudi for the celebration of a Mass, the singing of vespers, and a sermon on the saint's day, the 29th June.

The apothecary Slaw Gatt, who led the Qormi patriots during the rising against the French, lived close by.

THE JUSPATRONATI

The centre of village life in Malta and Gozo was, for centuries, the parish church. But the nobles and the rich, like the Knights, wished to build their own private chapels, often attached to their palaces.

The Church granted them the "juspatronatus", the right to nominate the rector.

58. St. Angelo, Martyr – Żejtun

E ntering Żejtun by the motor-road from Bir
id-Deheb one comes to Gregorio Bonnici Square,
and the church of St. Angelo.

The church was built in 1670 on a sober but
beautiful plan, possibly designed by the celebrated
Lorenzo Gafà. It was endowed by the Roman
Patrician Gregorio Bonnici, a Maltese nobleman, by
means of a contract drawn up in Rome and
published by Notary Antonio Giordano, secretary
and chancellor of the Regia Camera Apostolica on

the 4th January, 1765. The church was raised to the status of Abbey on the 4th April of the same year, and confirmed as such on 24th April by the Bishop of Malta, Mgr. Lorenzo Astiria. The founder, Gregorio Bonnici left the juspatronatus to the first-born among his successors. It is today held by the Testaferrata Bonici family.

The first abbot was Don Mario Testaferrata, nephew of the founder. When first built the church had a barrel vault and a dome. But after 170 years one of the side walls showed signs of weakness. Marquis Testaferrata renewed the three arches of the roof and the façade and pulled down the dome.

The front is imposing. Inside there are beautiful paintings by Giuseppe D'Arena. The main altar is ornamented and has a pair of finely sculptured side columns. There are two other altars.

In the sacristy there is an urn containing the remains of the Carmelite martyr, St. Angelo. It was received as a gift from Rome.

Before the war the feast of St. Rita used to be celebrated in this church.

Members of the Testaferrata family are buried here.

59. St. James – Luqa

The church is on the main road from Santa Lucija to the Airport. It has a belfry of unusual shape flanked by stone statues of St. Paul and St. James.

It was built around the year 1550, but was deconsecrated by Bishop Gargallo. The same Bishop reconsecrated it by decree dated 7th November, 1613, following a petition made by Peter Briffa and James Psaila. It was a juspatronatus of the Fiott family.

At the beginning of this century it was deconsecrated again, but at the request of Joseph

Ciappara it was given in juspatronatus to his family by means of a contract drawn up by Notary Francesco Giorgio Schembri on 27th October, 1901. Joseph Ciappara not only kept the chapel in good condition, but erected an apse and the belfry, and renewed the roof.

Joseph's son embellished it still further, among other things replacing the old titular painting, which had no artistic value, with one by R. Bonnici Calì. The procurator used to organise an attractive feast on the Sunday nearest to the 25th July.

A touching sign of the devotion of the Ciappara family to St. James is the fact that each of the six sons of Joseph Ciappara bore the second name of James. Another procurator was a James, all his sons having the second name James, and his grandson also a James.

During the second world war the Royal Malta Artillery gunners manning the nearby "St James" battery used to hear Mass in this church.

During a storm in 1979 a thunderbolt damaged the belfry.

The church is today neglected.

60. St. Lucy and St. Nicholas
– Buskett, Rabat

T his church is a juspatronatus of the Testaferrata
Viani family and is situated at Ġnien il-Far, on
the road from Buskett to Ġirgenti. It is dedicated to
St. Lucy and St. Nicholas of Bari. Originally there
were two churches which Bishop Dusina joined
together in 1575. It later collapsed but was rebuilt in
1706 by Anton Agius.

During the second world war it served as a
refugee centre. Among the refugees was a Rumanian
family. The fourteen-year old daughter of this family

was killed by splinters when a German bomb exploded nearby in 1941, damaging the church.

Up to 1960 the church was neglected. Then the Augustinian Fr. Raphael Azzopardi took the repairs in hand, paved and blessed it. For a time it was used by the Legion of Mary of Buskett for the holding of spiritual retreats. The place is ideal for retreats, being very quiet and secluded, with fragrant pine-trees breaking the monotony of the rocky neighbourhood.

In the years during which the chapel of St Anthony the Abbot attached to Verdala palace was closed to the public (q.v.) Sunday Mass was celebrated at this church.

Before the last war the Rabat clergy used to sing vespers and celebrate Mass on the feast days of St. Lucy and St. Nicholas. The practice has been discontinued, and the only activity still carried on is the teaching of the catechism.

The titular painting which was damaged during the raids was removed. It represented the Madonna and Child flanked by the titular saints. In a corner at the bottom there appeared the coat of arms of Anton Agius. The new painting is by Palmieri and represents St. Nicholas and St. Publius kneeling before Christ. Two smaller paintings are of St. Nicholas and St. Lucy respectively.

61. Our Lady "Tax-Xagħra" – Naxxar

KILIN

The word "xagħra" means a waste tract of land. Santa Marija, also knwon as "Our Lady of Graces", was built on such a barren rocky stretch, which in the last few decades has become a fashionable residential area.

The name could have originated from Xara, the name of some nobleman connected with the church. There used to hang in the sacristy a painting of a knight kneeling before the Virgin, with figures of souls in Purgatory at the bottom of the picture.

The church. which has a curious kind of bell-cot rising from the pediment, was built in 1500. As in the year 1690 it was in a very bad condition, it was rebuilt. But perhaps it was only repaired in that year because the date 1634 appears carved above the main painting.

The people of Naxxar held the church in considerable veneration. During carnival many people used to go there to recite the Rosary. Many Masses were celebrated and the sanctuary lamp was never allowed to go out. A curious custom during Lent was for the villagers to go to the church just after the mid-day meal to recite a special kind of Rosary when, instead of the Hail Mary the Our Father was said, and the Gloria was followed by the Kyrie and a Hail Mary.

The feast used to include decoration with damask hangings, the lighting of the front with coloured oil-lamps, and fireworks. The devotions used to last fifteen days. Today a Mass is celebrated on the 15th August. It is written in the archives of the parish church that: "this church, dedicated to Our Lady of Graces, or the Assumption of Sciara, celebrates the feast every year on the feast of the Assumption, with a sung Mass and vespers; other Masses are said on the feasts of St. Paul and St. Mary Magdalen, and on Saturdays the lamp is lit. The expenses are defrayed from contributions by the faithful and from a small capital possessed by the church."

The titular painting, by Zahra, has been taken to the parish church and hangs on the altar of the Assumption. It has been replaced by another painting. A leather altar frontal there was in this church is now kept in the Cathedral museum.

During the 1939/45 war soldiers were billeted in
Santa Marija. Holy Mass is celebrated on Sundays
and on one week-day.

62. The Immaculate Conception – Bengħisa

KILIN

This church is situated close to the Għar Ħasan road which branches off the Birżebbuġa - Ħal Far road.

It is a "juspatronatus", and was built in 1822 by master-mason Francis Callus, for Dun Ġakbu Gauċi of Żurrieq. In 1861-62 it was enlarged by the founder's nephew, Dun Ġużepp Callus. It was consecrated by Bishop Pace Forno in 1862.

It has one altar and a bell-cot with a big bell on which appears the name Concetta.

For thirty years it was under the care of Dun P.P. Saydon who used to say Mass in it. For more than another thirty years it was under the charge of his nephew, the renowned Prof. P.P. Saydon, who translated the Bible into Maltese.

63. The Assumption, Tas-Samra – Ħamrun

L ong before Hamrun was built there existed a
small chapel, dedicated to St. Nicholas, on Ta'
Braxia hill, close to the Valletta - Qormi road. It was
deconsecrated by Mgr. Dusina, in 1575. In the year
1630 it was rebuilt by Ġużè Casauri, who built beside
it rooms where he and his wife (Isabella Spinaci who,
as a baby in 1565, had been buried alive during a
bombardment by the besieging Turks) dwelt as
hermits until their deaths, which occurred
respectively in 1636 and 1646. The couple are buried

in the church as evidenced by a plaque and as reported by Mgr. Alpheran in his report of 1736.

Casauri, who used to travel frequently to Spain on business, acquired a copy of the famous Atocha Madonna of Madrid. He took the Atocha painting to the rebuilt church which since then began to be called the church of the "Samra" Madonna, samra meaning dark-skinned.

Mgr. Balaguer (1653) reports that many people used to visit the church, especially on Saturdays and on the 15th of each month. This devotion was revived in our times by the saintly Dun Ġorġ Preca, founder of the Society of Christian Doctrine. Adjoining the church is the home of the "Nuzzu" (Daughters of the Sacred Heart) nuns, who came to Malta in 1894.

During the French occupation (1798-1800) the Maltese insurgents bombarded Valletta from the Tas-Samra battery. The two guns embedded in the ground in front of the church are reminders of the event.

The church is a "lay juspatronatus" of the Borg Olivier family.

Besides the main altar there are altars dedicated to the Saints Joseph, Lawrence, Nicholas of Bari and Charles Borromeo. There are statues of St. Joseph, Our Lady of Sorrows, and the Sacred Heart of Jesus. The three bells from the Taylor foundry were consecrated on the 22nd June, 1947 by Archbishop Gonzi.

Masses are said daily, and spiritual exercises held during Lent. The feast is celebrated on the 15th August.

64. St. Paul Shipwrecked
– Xrobb il-Għaġin

This church was built in 1740. The tower close to it, called Bettina's tower, was built by the Marchioness Elizabeth Muscat Cassia D'Aurel. The church was restored in 1931 by the Marquis Angelo Muscat Cassia D'Aurel. It has one altar, a painting of St. Paul's shipwreck, and a smaller one of the Holy Family.

65. St. Simon – Wardija

This small but graceful neo-gothic church stands beside Qannotta Castle. It is a juspatronatus of the Depiro Gourgion family, owners of the castle which dominates the picturesque Qannotta valley.

Bishop Cagliares, in his pastoral report of 1616 wrote that it was deconsecrated. It is dedicated to the Apostle Simon, and was endowed with lands from the revenue of which the feast of St. Simon and St. Jude used to be celebrated on the 28th October.

During the time when it was neglected the titular painting was taken to the Sanctuary of Our Lady of Mellieħa, the rector of which sanctuary had the obligation to celebrate four masses on the feast day of the two apostles.

From the acts of Notary Matthew Cauchi (13th October 1629) it appears that a certain Salvatore Cauchi left a garden at Wardija, called "Calet il-Ħabib" as a foundation for the celebration of another Mass on the feast of St. Simon, and for the lighting of two lamps on Saturdays.

The sacristy adjoining the church was built some sixty years ago.

Up to the second world war Mass used to be celebrated frequently at St. Simon's.

In a niche under the bell-cot is a statue of the Madonna and Child. Statues of St. Peter and St. Paul stand at the two corners. The church is well kept. The titular painting shows St. Simon holding a saw.

66. St. Bartholomew – Rabat

The first church on the site of the present one was built around the year 1440 by Constantin Bartolo. His widow, Giovanna, by will dated 1451 in the acts of notary Sillato left the revenue from fields in the area of Tal-Ħandaq and Kwikipulli, for keeping alight the lamp at St. Bartholomew's. Moreover she left a small dwelling contiguous to the church for the use of "the man who lights the lamp." Later, Romana Bartolo, by will dated 10th October 1490 left a "laical juspatronatus" benefice to be enjoyed only by her descendants. A few years later one of the heirs, Fra Giovanni Bartolo, nicknamed Galeotto, became an Augustinian friar.

He ceded his right to the benefice in favour of the convent. On the strength of this cession the Augustinians presumed the right to nominate the subsequent beneficiaries. The Bartolo family disputed this, and the case ended before the ecclesiastical court which, in 1591, decided in favour of the family.

In 1601 Bishop Gargallo, in accordance with the decision taken in 1591, ordered that all who enjoyed prebends or benefices had to pay 5 per cent of them towards the building of the Jesuits' College. San Bert paid its share: three irbghajja per annum. (About 6 cents in today's currency).

The chapel was well kept in 1670, stated Bishop Molina in his report of the pastoral visit of that year. There was at the time the obligation to celebrate Mass every Sunday, and several Masses on the 24th August, the saint's feast-day. There was also the custom to endow, every year, a bride chosen by the Cumulo di Carità.

In 1798 it was in this church that the leader of the patriots, Notary Emanuele Vitale, organised the rising against the French. But someone had spied on the insurgents and reported them to Ludovico Savoya, rector of St. Paul's Grotto, and they had to look for another meeting-place.

Activity at St. Bartholomew's today is limited to the teaching of the catechism. The church was deconsecrated during the second world war.

67. St. Francis of Paola – Qormi

This fine church was built in 1706, beside the older chapel of the Annunciation (see sketch), during the time when Dun Silvestru Desira was parish priest of Qormi.

Francis Casha Cuschieri Testaferrata and his son Dun Ġorġ founded a benefice in favour of the priest taking care of the church.

By means of three decrees of the Sacred Congregation of Rites (20.9.1749, 30.8.1755 and 18.12.1756) the church became a lay juspatronatus of

he Casha family, one of the privileges being that
he descendants of the founders were to be buried
n the crypt. Many of the paintings are of saints after
whom members of the family were named in the
eighteenth century.

In 1798, the French soldiers passing through
Qormi stole all the silver articles they found in the
church and mutilated a large painting of the
Immaculate Conception. This painting was later
restored.

The church has two altars. The titular painting of
St. Francis of Paola is attributed to Francesco Zahra.

In the apse there is represented in gilt high relief
the Blessed Trinity. The side altar, on which stands a
statue of Our Lady of Lourdes, was once a privileged
altar. Two small paintings at the sides of the main
altar are of St. Louis Gonzaga and of the Immaculate
Conception. Other paintings are of St. Andrew, St.
Anne, St. Catherine, St. Mark and St. Matthew.
Another, of St. Anthony the Abbot, stands beside the
main door. Much revered is an Ecce Homo bust with
an indulgence granted by Bishop Labini on the 18th
December, 1787.

A Via Crucis made early this century is by Salvu
Scicluna. A portrait of Dun Ġorġ Casha, one of the
founders, hangs in the sacristy. Still preserved are
his priest's breviary, two volumes of the Horae
Diurnae printed shortly after 1670, and four missals
printed in Venice in 1681, 1728, 1731 and 1788. An
antiphonary is signed by Dun Anton Casha, parish
priest of Luqa from 1737 to 1759, with a note: "16th
August, 1766. I spent for this gradual 10 scudi and 5
tari."

The church is well cared for. Masses are celebrated for the repose of the souls of members of the founders' family, during the All Souls octave in November, and on the saint's feast day which falls on the 4th Sunday after Easter.

68. Saint Publius – Ta' Għammar, Gozo

The road from Ta' Pinu Basilica to the village of Għasri, skirting the Ta' Għammar hill on the north-western side, passes through the hamlet called, not very imaginatively, Wara ta'Għammar (behind Ta' Għammar). A narrow lane on the left-hand side of the road leads to the chapel.

There existed on this site an older church dedicated to St. Leonard, built by a certain George Tewma around the year 1550. Beside it was a cemetery. It was deconsecrated in 1654 by Bishop Balaguer Camarasa.

The present church was built in 1850 by Dun Ġużepp Cassar. Canon Theologian Dun Thomas Pace of the Cathedral laid the first stone on the 26th July of that year. The Archpriest of Għarb, Dun Salv Mizzi, representing the Bishop, blessed it on the 10th October 1852. The Archpriest of Għarb, Dun Publju Refalo, who died on 12th December, 1848, had expressed the wish that there should be at Ta' Għammar a church in honour of the Saint. The painting of St. Publius was given by the Mompalao family to the Archpriest on condition that the new church bear that name. Monsignor Publius Maria dei Conti Sant, who was Bishop of Malta and Gozo from 1848 to 1857 had expressed the same wish.

The two bells, named Paula and Publia, were installed on 16th April, 1967.

The floor of the church is paved with mosaic, and the dado is coated with the same material. The main altar, naturally, is dedicated to St. Publius. There is on the side a small niche with a statue of Our Lady of Lourdes, and there are statuettes of the Ecce Homo and of Our Lady of the Legion of Mary. Other paintings are of St. Anthony of Padua, Our Lady of Sorrows, the Assumption, the Blessed Hearts of Jesus and Mary and of St. Leonard, Abbot, patron of slaves. There is a small sacristy, an attractive Via Crucis, and benches for the faithful.

The Rosary, daily, the Via Crucis and other devotions are recited. The church is well cared for by the young women of the Legion of Mary. A special function is held on the feast day which falls on the third or fourth Sunday after the Epiphany.

69. Saint Mark – Siġġiewi.

KILIN

This church was built in the year 1608 by Francesco Mamo, but it is said that there existed an earlier one on the same site.

The main painting shows Our Lady flanked by St. Mark (and lion!) and St. Francis. There are statues of Our Lady of Fatima and of St. Nicholas. The harmonium was a gift of Gaspare Pace.

Mass is celebrated on all weekdays and the Rosary is recited daily. On Christmas eve the M.U.S.E.U.M. (Society of Christian Doctrine) children sing carols before and after a sermon delivered by one of them.

On the 25th April, St. Mark's day, a sung Mass is celebrated.

In the past the Rogation processions, now suppressed, used to start from this church and proceed to the Parish Church. Peasants considered this procession a prayer for a good wheat harvest. According to an old Maltese saying: "he who prays for rain on St. Mark's day prays for fire from heaven."

The Legion of Mary hold their meeting at St. Mark's.

70. Saint Michael – Salini, Burmarrad

This church, which stands off the Regional Road as it sweeps past the Kennedy Memorial, was built in the year 1652. It used to serve the people of the Qawra and l-Imdawra areas, but since the building of the Burmarrad church is has lost its importance.

Shortly after it was built, Girolama, wife of Antonio Zammit of Naxxar, made a foundation for a sung Mass and a sermon on the feast day of St. Michael, and for the singing of first vespers on the eve. (*Acts of Notary Cauchi of 1659*)

After the last war the M. U. S. E. U. M. society used to hold meetings at St. Michael's .

There is one altar dedicated to St. Michael and a Via Crucis, with a fine Via Crucis cross. The Franciscans who serve the new parish of Burmarrad have renewed the pavement and installed an iron door. The bell, unfortunately, has been stolen.

The festa is celebrated on the last Sunday in September, when a pilgrimage procession goes from the parish church to St. Michael's, and a Mass with a homily is celebrated.

71. St. Lucy – Gozo

The church is in the hamlet of Santa Lucija, not very far from Kerċem.

It is very old. A much older one which existed on the same site was deconsecrated in 1544, and Mgr Dusina deconsecrated it again in 1575. It was deconsecrated yet again in 1657, but after a time it was rebuilt by Canon Mikelanġ Dandalone who lived nearby. When the building was completed Dun Mikelanġ claimed that he ought to be the first rector, particularly because he was also rector of the canonry called "tal-knejjes rurali". But Archpriest Cassar of the Cathedral did not agree. The matter was referred to Rome, but by the time a decision arrived both contestants had died. Since that time the church has been served by a priest nominated by the Bishop to say Mass on Sundays and Feast Days and to preach, teach the catechism and hear confessions.

From the 8th October, 1848 till November 1851, St. Lucy church served as vice-parish church. There was beside it a small house for the "Viċendarju" who was paid a pension from the benefice called "Ta' Carbuni" in Malta. Although small the church is very graceful, and has a cupola and a central bell-tower. It has three altars and three old paintings showing respectively St. Lucy with the Madonna of the Snows, St. Peter and St. Paul, and the flight into Egypt. There is an organ gallery. The church and sacristy were enlarged by the rector, Dun Anton Grima. On 5th December, 1948 four new bells cast by the firm of John Taylor were blessed by Bishop Pace. They bear the names of Ġużeppa, Pawla, Luċija and Mikelina.

On the 9th November, 1952 the church and the main altar were consecrated by Bishop Pace.

Other improvements include a marble main altar, twelve paintings by Briffa, decorations by the painter Alfred Camilleri, statues of St. Lucy, the Sacred Heart and St. Thomas, and silk damask coverings for the walls.

The festa is held on the Sunday after the 13th December. Mass is said daily by the rector.

72. St. Anthony of Padua
– Ix-Xagħra, Marsascala

Situated between three parishes: Żejtun, Żabbar and Marsascala, this church used to form part of the Żejtun Parish but now is within the Marsascala (Wied il-Għajn) limits. It is known as Tal-Latmija, and can be reached either by a lane which branches left from the Żejtun - Ramla road bypassing the church of St Mary of Ħal Tmiem, or from the Marsascala - Żabbar bypass.

It was built by Dun Andrea Polladino. (*Acts of Notary M.A. Attard dated 12 th February, 1675*).

The main painting, by an unknown artist, shows tha Madonna with St. Philip Neri and St. Anthony. A smaller painting represents the Saviour.

A statuette of St. Anthony which has a ring attached to the back of the neck is kept in this chapel. It used to be taken out to sea by fishermen who lowered it attached to the tunny net while reciting a prayer for a good catch. It was also lowered down wells in time of drought.

When the church still formed part of the Żejtun parish, the feast of St. Anthony was celebrated by the Żejtun clergy with a High Mass and a sermon. The place used to be beflagged, coloured oil lamps were lit, and the Beland Band played, It was quite an attractive festa attended by a large number of people.

The church is now used for spiritual retreats.

73. Our Lady of Carmel – Ta' Ħamet, Gozo

KILIN

This church is situated in the fertile plain between Xagħra and Xewkija, on the road joining these two villages, but within the parochial limits of Victoria.

It is a "Lay juspatronatus", built in 1835 by Liberat Grech, a farmer who, in 1798, had been nominated head of the Gozitan armed forces fighting the French occupiers by Archpriest Cassar of Rabat. It was blessed on 1st January, 1837 by Canon Dun Saver Grech, son of the founder.

The titular painting of Our Lady of Mount Carmel, by Tommaso Madiona, was carried in solemn procession from the church of Xewkija, accompanied by the Cathedral Chapter, on the 22nd July, 1838.

Two side altars are respectively dedicated to the Crucifix and St. Michael. The altarpiece of the latter was done in 1844 by Antonio Falzon.

The main altar was originally of stone, but a marble one made by the Barsanti firm of Carrara, was set up in 1952.

The twin belfries were erected in 1958 by Karlu Vella of Kerċem, working under Mr. Damato.

The church was consecrated by Bishop Mgr. Giuseppe Pace on the 26th July, 1954.

In 1950 there was installed a lovely statue of Our Lady of Fatima, which had been crowned by Pope Pius XII. Father Joseph Mizzi, who was then rector of the church, spread the devotion to Our Lady of Fatima throughout Gozo.

The feast of Our Lady of Carmel is celebrated on the 16th July. The apparitions of Fatima are also commemorated with considerable devotion on the 13th day of the six months from May to October.

74. Saint Margaret
– Għajn Riħana, Burmarrad

This very old church was rebuilt by Canon Dun Nerik de Bordino, who bequeathed it to the Cathedral. The curator nominated by the Cathedral Chapter had the obligation of celebrating Mass in it on the feast day of St. Margaret of Antioch, and to provide food for those who attended the said Mass. The procurator used to celebrate the feast independently of the Parish of Naxxar within the limits of which it was situated.

In 1658 Bishop Balaguer deconsecrated it, but it was not long before it was reintegrated. The heirs of

Blas Bezzina used to light the lamp on Saturdays and pay for a Mass on the feast day and the singing of first vespers on the eve. Dominic Bezzina bound himself to pay for the celebration of twelve Masses during the year. (*Acts of Notary Matthew Cauchi of the 14th October, 1666*)

The front half of the church was added in 1849. The plaque one sees on the front of many country churches with the wording "non gode l'immunità ecclesiastica" can be seen inside the church, on the outer wall of the old half. The plaque warned people fleeing from justice that they were not to expect immunity by taking shelter inside that particular church.

A sacristy and an upper room were added, and in 1850 Dr. Michael Bellanti painted the beautiful titular painting, which in 1977 was ably restored by Miss M.R. Borg Olivier. Previously there was a painting by Zahra, in a very bad condition.

In 1866 another room which served as a kitchen, was added. The façade was built anew in 1882. There is one bell, made in 1708 on which appear the figures of the Crucifix and St. Publius.

A small stone font is similar to the one at the Ħal Millieri church.

The church was extensively renovated some twenty years ago when it was under the care of the Rev. Dr. Frank Grech, S.J., helped by a Żejtun pensioner Anġlu Carabott. Brother Joseph Spiteri, S.J. restored an old set of engravings of the Via Crucis which were in a very bad state. Also of interest is a bas-relief of the Madonna, on wood, made by a twelve year old boy, who died shortly after finishing it.

75. Our Lady of Light – Żebbuġ

KILIN

This is one ot the finest of the smaller churches. It was built in 1738 at the request of two priests, Jerome Azzopardi and Horace Xiberras. The architect was Lorenzo Gafà. It was blessed in 1740.

On the same site there existed an older church dedicated to the Visitation of Our Lady to St. Elizabeth, which was deconsecrated by Mons. Balaguer in the year 1657. To commemorate its existence a small painting of the Visitation was placed above the titular painting of the new church, which bears the inscription: "in you we see the light."

The church has one stone altar. There are paintings of the Saints Liborius, Sebastian, Nicholas, Simeon, Mary Magdalen, and of the Transfiguration. There is all that is needed for the sacred service, such as vestments, candlesticks, etc. Recent additions are a new door, benches, a new pavement, a marble dado and a table altar. The paintings have been restored and the roof painted.

In the elegant belfry are two bells. This belfry, and other parts of the church were considerably damaged on the 2nd May, 1941 by the explosion of a parachute mine.

The church enjoyed a "directurn dominium" on fields at "Ta' Xagħret il-Għar" and at "ta' Xoqq u Diha" which between them yielded the revenue of fifteen scudi and six tari, sufficient for the celebration of the festa of Our Lady of Light, on the second Sunday in November, and that of Our Lady of Patronage, with first and second vespers, a sung Mass and the lighting of the sanctuary lamp.

This church is held in great veneration by the people of the neighbourhood who have always contributed generously for all its needs.

76. St. Philip Neri – Għaxaq

This church was built in 1761-62 by Dun Ġwann Filippu Żammit, on his own property, the architect being Bastjan Saliba who built the parish church of Għaxaq as well. The founder blessed St. Philip's on the 29th May, 1763.

Dun Ġwann was a keen sportsman who used to go out shooting before saying Mass. This did not please the parish priest who ordered the sacristan to close the doors of the church to keep him out. But Dun Ġwann had friends among the Knights of St.

John, and with their help obtained for the church of St. Philip the privilege of affiliation to the basilica of St. John Lateran, thereby placing it under the jurisdiction of the Roman Basilica. Not even the Bishop could now claim any rights on it. The church became a Basilica in 1769. The main painting was done in 1763. Dun Ġwann died in 1782 and is buried in his church.

77. St. Domenica – Dingli

KILIN

One of the ten parishes mentioned in 1436 in Bishop Senatore de Mello's report was that of Ħal Tartarni, a small village close to the lands of "Djar il-Bniet" the property of the Desguanez family. The first parish church was that of the old St. Domenica, which once stood near the site of the present church of that name. Later, Hal Tartarni was joined to another hamlet to form the present village of Ħad-Dingli.

The present church of St. Domenica was built by Baron Marcantonio Inguanez and his wife Monica, by decree dated 25th February, 1669. It thus became a juspatronatus of his family in perpetuity.

The church which has one stone altar was neglected and during the last war was occupied by the military. After the war, at a time when Dun Ġwann Azzopardi was rector, it was repaired by Baroness Chesney Sceberras D'Amico Inguanez. The present owner, Baron D'Amico Inguanez Apap Bologna, has recently caused the titular painting to be renovated.

The feast is celebrated on a day in July with the celebration of a Mass.

78. Our Lady "Ta' l-Abbandunati" – Wardija

"Ta' l-Abbandunati" means "of the abandoned". But this chapel is certainly not abandoned or in any way neglected.

It is built on the hill called "tal-Ballut" (the oaks) opposite the "hotba tas-sultan" (the king's knoll), and commands a magnificent view of St. Paul's Bay. Contiguous to it is the "palazz tas-sultan", so called because it was the favourite haunt of the Bailiff Perellos y Roccaful, who later on was elected Grand Master of the Order of St. John, reigning from 1697 to 1720. Earlier there had been on this spot a garden owned by the Vicar General Tolessanti.

The church was blessed by Vicar General Dun Antonio Manso on the 18th April, 1690. Perellos, who hailed from Aragón, placed in it a painting by Stefano Erardi, a copy of the renowned Nuestra Señora de los Desamparados, Our Lady of those without shelter, or protection, venerated in Valencia.

On the 13th June, 1798, the soldiers of Napoleon wreaked havoc in the little church, as they did in other churches. They carried away all the valuables they could carry, silver objects, precious stones, even the silver frames of the Via Crucis. They removed the Erardi painting from its frame, cast it outside the church, smeared dirt on it and slit the "throats" of the Madonna and Child. The shocked peasants of the neighbourhood recovered the painting which was then restored. But the gashes in the canvas were still ugly. It was restored again by Chev. Vincenzo Bonello.

The church is a juspatronatus of the Piscopo Macedonia Żamitt family. The late Count Bernardo dedicated himself to its embellishment, spending money lavishly. He enlarged the chapel, building three sacristies so that worshippers would find shelter in rough weather. (Quite in tune with the Desamparados ideal). He built the cupola and a large bell-tower having five perfectly tuned bells; installed a walnut pulpit, and paved the floor with marble. He finally caused two statues to be placed on either side of the door, on the outside. One is of St. Bernard, his patron saint, and the other of St. Michael, whose feast falls on his birthday. (I once jokingly observed to him that St. Michael is my patron saint, and I was born on the 20th August, St. Bernard's day!).

Mass is clebrated on Saturdays and Sundays, on feast days and on the first Friday of each month. Spiritual Exercises are held during Advent and Lent. A festa is held at Christmas. During the last week in Lent the statue of Our Lady of Sorrows is carried in procession.

The feast is celebrated on the last Sunday in June. In the past, three bands used to play marches, and fireworks were let off. Up to sixty members of the fraternities, from Wardija, Mosta, St. Paul's Bay and Rabat used to take part in the procession. It used to be a very popular festa.

79. Our Lady of Sorrows – Żebbuġ

This church, a juspatronatus of the Bonnici Mallia
family, was built by Dr. Baldassarre Debono,
M.D. early in the eighteenth century. At his request
it received the honour of the title of Basilica affiliated
to St. John Lateran. It enjoys the same privileges of
the Roman basilica and is independent of the diocese
of Malta. It passed to the Bonnici family when
Francesca Romana Debono, (the granddaughter of
Baldassarre who was exiled by the Knights of St.
John for his part in the Mannarino plot), married Dr.

Giuseppe Maria Bonnici. This doctor was the last Ħakem of Mdina. He was appointed Regent of Mdina and its dependencies by the British. That is why the Bonnici family, as well as the church of Our Lady of Sorrows, are still known in Żebbuġ by the name of "Tar-reġġent".

This very graceful church, adjoining which are two sacristies, has a set of bells, a marble altar, a painting of Our Lady, probably the work of Antoine de Favray, a marble pavement, silver candlesticks, cross and reliquaries, an organ made in Italy around the year 1700 and still functioning, and everything required for the religious service. In one of the sacristies hangs a framed list of the names of the owners and the date of their deaths, namely: Dr. Baldassarre Debono, Nicholas Debono, Francesca Romana and her husband Dr. Giuseppe Maria Bonnici J.U.D., Paul Maria Bonnici, Giuseppe Maria Bonnici, Carmela Bonnici Mallia and her Brother Giovanni, LL.D., respectively father and uncle of the present owner, Joseph Bonnici Mallia, L.C. There are also three small paintings: those on either side of the titular painting representing St. Nicholas of Tolentino and the twin saints Cosmas and Damian; and the third, which hangs above the main door, shows the Three Kings, one of whom was called Balthasar.

The proprietor of the church nominates the rector and the sacristan. The rector celebrates Mass on the anniversary of the death of each owner, on the seven main feasts of Our Lady, and on the feasts of St. John the Baptist, Saints Cosmas and Damian, St. Nicholas of Tolentino, St. Joseph and Saint Paul. On

Fridays the rector and the sacristan sing the Stabat Mater.

The titular feast is properly celebrated on the Friday preceding Good Friday. The Żebbuġ clergy take part together with a good number of the faithful. At the termination of the first vespers, on the eve of the feast, a reception used to be held in the larger of the two sacristies, in which the owner's family, their friends and the singers took part.

80. Our Lady of Victories – Mtaħleb

KILIN

This church stands on the edge of a cliff in one of the most picturesque spots in Malta.

A much older church existed on the same site. In January, 1575, Mgr. Dusina, the Apostolic Visitor, reported that he found it in a very bad state. At that time it was called The Assumption of Our Lady of Monte Calibbo.

In 1607, Gio Vincenzo Castelletti rebuilt it from the foundations, changed its name to that of the Nativity of Our Lady, and endowed it with a

juspatronatus of eight scudi a year for the celebration
of thirteen masses, one on the feast day, and one on
the first Sunday of each month. (*Acts of Notary Andrea
Allegretto, 5th May, 1607*)

The church, which is a juspatronatus of the
D'Amico Inguanez family, was rebuilt in 1656 by
Andreotta Castelletti, the husband of Isabella Saura,
daughter of the philantropist Nicola. He paid for the
titular painting, done by Pereira, which represents
St. Anne with the baby Madonna, surrounded by St.
Andrew, St. Thomas Aquinas, the Guardian Angel
and, in a bottom corner, Andreotta himself.

Another foundation for the celebration of twenty
masses on feasts of obligation was made by baroness
Maria Teresa D'Amico Inguanez in 1869. (*Acts of
Notary Vincenzo Caruana*)

Dun Vincenzo Mangani became rector in 1913. In
1948 he decided to enlarge the church, but died the
same year. As the titular painting was in a bad sate
he asked his foster-son Karmenu Said to restore it.
Said, who was a restorer at the Museum did a very
good job in spite of various technical difficulties. The
painting was restored again in 1983 by G. Farrugia,
the work this time involving the transference of the
paint to a fresh canvas.

The enlargement of the church, begun by Fr.
Mangani was continued by Canon Dun Karm Cefai
who succeeded him as rector. The work was carried
out under the direction of Ġużè Damato who
charged no fees for his services. The expenses of the
building were borne by the Mtaħleb farmers. The
church now has two side altars surmounted by
paintings of St. Paul and St. Joseph the Worker, both

done by C. Spiteri. Paul and Francesca Żahra of Mtaħleb paid for the main altar and Karmenu Cutajar for a marble table altar. Other farmers paid for the marble pavement and the tabernacle, also in marble, made by the firm of Salvu Muscat according to a design by Carmelo Tonna. (*Mr. Tonna was my drawing master way back in the twenties. R.I.P.*)

A popular festa is held every year. On the eve folk singers from various parts of the island congregate at Mtaħleb. The following day a fair is held, in which the Count Roger Band of Rabat takes part. Seventy years ago only a small number of bandsmen, about fifteen in all, led by euphonium player Pawlu Cortis used to play. I was one of them, banging away on the side-drum! It was a lovely festa, humble and intimate, unlike the noisy crowded festas of the big towns.

Masses are celebrated on Sundays and Festas, on the first Fridays and Saturdays of each month. From October to Easter Mass is celebrated daily. The farmers have contributed generously for the frequent celebration of Masses, the adoration of the Eucharist, and for the spiritual exercises during Lent.

81. Our Lady "of the Letter"
– Binġemma

This graceful church is perched on the edge of the rocky side of the very picturesque valley down which the road descends from the heights of Binġemma to Mġarr.

It was built in 1690 by the family of Count Sant. It is popularly known as "ta' l-ittra" (of the letter). Ferres refers to it by the name of 'B.V. de Sacra Littera". This name is probably a corruption of "ta' Itria" a title by which Our Lady is venerated in nearby Sicily.

In the report of Bishop Molina's pastoral visit of 1680 there is a reference to a church of Our Lady of Isdria, situated in a garden at Binġemma, the procurators of which used to celebrate Mass and sing the first vespers on the feast-day. It was deconsecrated in 1657 but reopened in 1680, after a certain Stanislaw endowed it with funds, and blessed on 11 th May, 1681 by the Bishop's Vicar, Ludovico Famucelli. It had a yearly income of twenty scudi. Depicted in the titular painting, by Stefano Erardi, were the saints Paul, Dominic, Roque, Francis of Assisi, and Anton. This painting has been removed to St Agatha's in Rabat.

Fr. Francis Xavier Schembri, M.S.S.P., who for several years said Mass in this church told me that as far as he knew the name of the chapel was "ta' Itria". He added that it had been built after an older one had collapsed. It is likely, then, that Bishop Molina's report (1680) referred to the old church, and that the new church was built ten years later, after he had left Malta, when he was appointed bishop of Lérida.

The roof of the church is a ribbed barrel vault. Under the round window above the door is the coat of arms of Bishop David Cocco Palmeri (1681-1711). The said coat of arms appears also on the titular painting which shows Our Lady and Child, enthroned, with two Franciscan Friars, a Dominican and a Jesuit. Obviously this is not the canvas described by Molina, who was Cocco Palmeri's predecessor.

A marble plaque above the door on the inside confirms that the name of the chapel is Our Lady of

Itria. It seems that devotion to the Madonna under this title was fairly strong in Malta, because an altar dedicated to her is to be seen at the Dominican church in Valletta.

Below the church is a cave consisting of three chambers, the innermost of which is a late Roman grave. On the opposite side of the valley are several rock-cut caves, varied in shape and size. They are called "the caves of the Jews".

The church is well cared for by the priests of the Missionary Society of St. Paul who celebrate Mass in it on Sundays at 6.30a.m.

82. St. Philip
and St. James
– Tal-Balal, Birkirkara

This church was built in 1733 by Dun Gaspare Giuseppe Vassallo, who was the provost (propostu) of the Collegiate Basilica of Birkirkara. It is still called "tal- Propostu".

The founder dedicated the church to the Apostles Philip and James and the souls in Purgatory. He wished to provide a place where the inhabitants of the area would be able to assist at Mass on Sundays and festas. He provided all the vestments and accessories required for the sacred service, and obtained relics of St. James, St. Philip, and other saints. He left a legacy for the lighting of the sanctuary lamp on all Saturdays, for the celebration of the feast in honour of the two apostles, and for the celebration of Mass on all Sundays of the summer months.

Unfortunately he could not find a man ready to undertake the duties of sacristan because no one would take on such duties without the right to enjoy the exemptions and privileges of the ecclesiastical court. The Sacra Congregazione had issued a decree whereby sacristans of country churches enjoyed ecclesiastical immunity only if not less than two Masses a week were said in the church where they served.

Provost Vassallo wrote to Rome to explain that because of this difficulty no priest could say Mass at Tal-Balal, and that consequently religious practice in the area was declining. The Bishop endorsed the petition that the sacristan of this church ought to enjoy the exemptions and privileges of the ecclestiastical court. The Congregation approved the request.

In 1798 the French invaders abolished ecclesiastical immunity, and on the 10th April, 1828, the British Governor by proclamation removed all ecclesiastical jurisdiction except in religious law-suits. The ecclesiastical immunity of churches was also abolished, and marble plaques with the words "Non gode l'immunità ecclesiastica" were placed on the door-jambs of most country churches. (A wag once translated the Italian words into: "no good lemonade here!") The Government sought the confirmation of the Holy See. Pope Leo XII did not give it, but the law was passed all the same.

For a long time the church was used as a store.

It has now been restored by the Ministry of the Environment and the San Ġwann Civic Council. Members of the Lyceum Old Boys Association meet in it for the celebration of Mass three times a year. They propose to instal a copy of the titular painting, which has been removed to the Parish church of San Gwann.

83. St. John the Baptist – Naxxar

KILIN

This church, situated half-way between Naxxar and Mosta, is quite old. In 1575 Mons. Dusina reported that it did not even possess a door. He therefore ordered Paul Borg and John Zarb, who were voluntarily paying for the celebration of Masses, to provide a wooden door within two weeks on pain of a fine of fifteen scudi or the suspension of the Masses!

In 1615 the church enjoyed an annual rental of three tarì to be spent on the celebration of Mass on the feast day. The sanctuary lamp had to be lit every Thursday by the heirs of Joseph Sammut who had bequeathed an annuity for a period of sixty years. On 14th April, 1659 Bishop Balaguer deconsecrated the church, and its revenues as well as the main painting were transferred to the parish church. It was not long after this, however, that St. John's reopened for religious services. It is evident from the architecture that this was not the first church to be built on the site. The present one seems to date from the seventeenth century. The titular painting, donated by Dun James Casha, who was parish priest of Naxxar from 1720 to 1745, is probably the work of Francesco Zahra. Four smaller canvases, copies of the Preti paintings in St. John's Co-Cathedral represent episodes in the life of the Baptist. Above the main door there is also a small painting of the Visitation. This painting was formerly under the titular. It was removed in 1940 to make place for a relic of St. Pacificus given to the Naxxar parish priest, Dun E. Micallef by Canon Caruana Gatto of St. Paul's in Valletta. It had been carried in procession by the Naxxar clergy from the church of Santa Lucija, another of the lovely small churches to be found in Naxxar. The marble altar was installed in the year 1801 and other important maintenance works were carried out in the thirties of this century, by procurator Gerald Sciberras.

This church was never really abandoned. In 1730 Joseph Frendo donated a field from the rents of which the saint's feast could be celebrated, with the singing of vespers, a High Mass, and also for the lighting of the lamp on Saturdays. (*Acts of Notary*

Joseph Gatt). And in 1751 Dun John Baptist Mifsud
left the usufruct of a house in Narrow Street, Naxxar,
for the same purpose and for the preaching of a
panegyric and the celebration of two Masses. The
celebration of Masses was frequent.

For a time during the last war refugees were
housed in St. John's. For a long time the Blessed
Sacrament was kept in it, the Rosary and the Via
Crucis were recited daily, and the saintly Dun Ġorġ
Preca used to hold conferences for the M.U.S.E.U.M.
Society, as he was wont to do in other small chapels
away from the noise and the distractions of the city.

On the feast day, the 24th of June, the church used
to be lit with coloured oil lamps. How magically
beautiful were those lamps before the advent of the
garish electric lighting!

There is the custom, probably originating in
Spain, to light bonfires on the eve of the feast of St.
John the Baptist. (It is a convenient way of disposing
of old furniture!) The bonfire in front of Naxxar's St.
John was something enormous, the pile of fire-wood
at times rising to a height of several feet. Another
quaint custom was for little girls to carry dolls to St.
John's in imitation of the Christening ceremony. A
procession with the Blessed Sacrament proceeds from
the Parish Church to St. John's on the feast of the
Sacred Heart, the week after Corpus Christi.

There is a revival of religious activity in this
church. Mass is celebrated daily, something the
inhabitants of the new housing estate find very
convenient. The Rosary, too is recited daily, and from
time to time retreats by various religious
organisations are held.

VOWS

Several small churches, as well as wayside shrines, were built in fulfilment of vows or in thanksgiving for graces received.

84. Christ the Redeemer – Għaxaq

T he building of this church began in October 1852, and was completed in September, 1859.

According to a popular story, a certain Mikelanġ Żammit, a land surveyor from Għaxaq, in the year 1806 when he was at Żurrieq, listened to a sermon on the Passion of Our Lord and was so impressed that he decided to build a niche in honour of the Redeemer. But he forgot all about it, until one day while riding on Kalamia hill he fell off the horse and injured himself. Taking this as a reminder, instead of one niche he built two, the second one being in honour of the Veronica. The Redeemer niche is by Paolo Azzopardi a pupil of the sculptor Mariano Gerada.

Years later, Dun Ġużepp Demicoli, seeing that many people used to go and pray at the Redeemer niche, decided to build a church. The designer was Franġisk Carabott of Żejtun. The building cost 12,000 scudi. The statue in the niche was transported to the church and placed on the main altar. Other statues are of St. John the Evangelist and of Our Lady of Sorrows. In the sacristy there are many *ex votos*.

The feast is celebrated on the first Friday in July. Franciscan Sisters who since 1939 have taken care of the church celebrate another feast in honour of St. Francis of Assisi in October.

85. St. Clement – Żejtun

Clement Tabone built this church in the year 1658. This date appears on the door. Tabone built the church to fulfil a vow he made when he was attacked by a band of marauding Turks as he was riding past this place. He bound himself to provide all that was needed for the divine service, to celebrate the feast on the Saint's day (the 23rd November) with a Mass and sung vespers, to light the lamp every Saturday, and to pay for the celebration of two Masses every week for the repose of the soul of his wife Dorothy

Cumbo. (*Acts of Notary Salvatore Ciantar*) All this was
to be paid out of rents from two fields he possessed
at "Tal-Bur" and "Tal-Ħofra" in Delimara. (*Notary
Julian Felici of 13th August 1667*)

There are in the church two good paintings. The
titular, in which Tabone himself is portrayed, is by
Stefano Erardi. A smaller one is by Żahra.

The church, paved some thirty years ago, is well
kept. In the middle of the pavement there is a grave.
The altar stands higher than is normal, the reason
being that after a heavy downpour the church is
often flooded.

St. Clement's is a sub-parish church.

86. St. Agatha – Żurrieq

This church is situated on the Żurrieq - Ħal Far road in an area known, appropriately enough, as "Ta' Sant'Agti."

An older church was built on this site in the sixteenth century. On the 24th November, 1658, Bishop Balaguer deconsecrated it. In 1854, Ċikku Grixti, called "ta' Katita", rebuilt it at the request of a woman who wished thereby to fulfil a vow. The new church, smaller than the old one, was blessed on 27th February, 1859 by the Vicar General, Mons.

Philip Amato, at the time of the first pastoral visit of Bishop Pace Forno.

During the second world war, the Benedictine Father Rutledge, who was later to die in the invasion of Sicily, used to say Mass and look after the spiritual needs of the British soldiers stationed in the vicinity.

Father Saviour Farrugia, who when still a seminarian had been appointed procurator of St. Agatha's, enlarged the church in 1952, paved it, and bought a Via Crucis and new vestments.

The painting, by an unknown artist, was restored by Chev. R. Bonnici Calì.

The feast is celebrated on the Sunday following the 5th of February.

87. Our Lady of Ħal Tmiem – Żejtun

Not far from St. Gregory's, on the road to St. Thomas' Bay, a lane leads to this typical country chapel: squat, with a small bell-cot and barred windows.

Above the door there is carved a white eight-pointed cross on blue ground, and close to it the date 1597. It was in that year that the chapel was built by Leonardo Tabone of the hamlet of Bisqallin. Ħal Tmiem was probably another small hamlet which has disappeared.

In the acts of Notary Andrea Attard, dated 12th September, 1628, Leonardo Tabone left a benefice of moneys, derived from the rents of three fields, with which every year a poor girl was to receive her dowry. One year the beneficiary was to be chosen from Bisqallin, and the following year from Birgu, where Leonardo's wife was born. The wedding had to be celebrated on the feast of the Assumption, at the church of Ħal Tmiem, and during the twelve days preceding the marriage the bride-to-be was obliged to pray for Leonardo's family.

The back part of the church was hit during the war. Unfortunately when it was repaired the damaged part was roofed over with concrete instead of being rebuilt in the style of the rest of the chapel, with Norman arches and stone slabs.

At Santa Marija Mass is celebrated daily.

88. Saint John the Evangelist
– Baħar iċ-Ċagħak

The sketch of this church is a copy of one I made some forty years ago. Since then St. John's has become surrounded by large buildings.

According to Achille Ferres it was built early in the eighteenth century in fulfilment of a vow made by a rich person from Għargħur who barely escaped capture and enslavement by Barbary corsairs. It seems that an ex-slave of his had given the tip to the marauders. Ferres does not give the name of this person, but in the acts of Notary Giuseppe Debono, a certain cleric, Giovanni Portelli, had left a bequest for the celebration of Masses on the feast of St. John the Evangelist and for the distribution of some hazelnuts to those who attended, and for another Mass on the feast of St. Lawrence. Up to some forty years ago the sung Mass used to be celebrated by the Għargħur clergy. Canon Amabile Camilleri of Valletta wrote to me once that he had said Mass three times at St. John's and had received his handful of hazelnuts.

The small chapel is octagonal. The titular painting shows St. John and the Immaculate Conception, and bears the date 1757. Carved above it is an eagle (symbol of St. John the Evangelist) and the Madonna monogram. At the sides are paintings of St. Paul and St. Lawrence, and the Portelli coat of arms.

A new Via Crucis has replaced an old engraved one which has been taken to the library of the Franciscan Friars Minor, of Valletta, for safe keeping. On the back of one of the prints is an inscription to the effect that the Via Crucis, a gift of Giuseppe Pullicino, son of Dr. Arcangelo, was blessed by the superior of the Franciscans of Rabat on the 16th September, 1872.

Close to the chapel is a house where the students of the Franciscan convent of Rabat used to spend the summer vacations, and presumably hear Mass at St. John's. The Franciscans took over the chapel in 1947. In 1959 they started building the Portiuncola House, which soon became an important centre for retreats.

Mass is said at this chapel daily. The stone altar has been removed and a table altar installed instead.

As Bahar iċ-Ċagħak is fast becoming a popular
residential area, the Franciscans are building a larger
church dedicated to Our Lady of the Angels not far
from St. John's.

89 St. Catherine – Mqabba

W here the church of St. Catherine now stands there were originally two churches, built in 1550, dedicated to St. Peter and St. Catherine. They fell into disrepair and on the 13th October, 1759 Bishop Rull ordered their demolition. In their place one church was rebuilt under the names of the two saints. The first stone was laid by Parish Priest Giovanni Battista Torricelli, the Bishop's delegate, in August 1764. Relics of the martyr saints Candidus, Agnes and Columba, and a medal with the image of

St. Peter and St. Paul, were buried under the first stone. Ten years later, the same priest, with the permission of Bishop Pellerano, blessed the new church.

Up to sixty years ago the church was in regular use, with penitential processions on the first of January and on the feasts of St. Peter and St. Catherine, with the celebration of Masses and the singing of vespers. The feast of St. John the Evangelist was also celebrated. The church now serves as a store for festa decorations.

The titular painting, done in 1776 shows Our Lady and Child with St. Catherine, St. John the Evangelist and an unknown praying person presumably the donor. The letters V.F.G.A. indicate that this was a votive offering.

THE GUILDS

The religious guilds, fore-runners of the trade unions, first appeared in the ninth century and looked after the material, social and spiritual interests of craft workers and merchants.

In Malta they were called "fratellanzi", (brotherhoods). The members of a particular craft helped each other financially, ensured that a fair price was paid for their work and products, but ensured also that the products were of good quality. They instructed their apprentices in the craft, the apprentice being bound to serve his master until he himself could produce his "masterpiece" which earned him the title and status of "mgħallem", a master craftsman.

Each "fratellanza " had its patron saint and took part in religious processions, behind its own standard, wearing a mozzetta of distinctive colour over a well-creased white tunic. This habit is called "kunfratija ", probably a corruption of the Spanish "Cofradía", which means "brotherhood" and also "trade union."

Among the oldest "fratellanzi" are those of St. Joseph (carpenters) of Rabat and Birgu. St. Cyprian was the patron saint of shoemakers; St. Demetrius of caulkers; St. Omobonus of tailors; St. Andrew, fishermen, etc.

In time the "fratellanzi" became purely religious, each dedicated to a particular service. Thus the "Charity" fraternity of Valletta, and that of St. Peter and Paul of Nadur, helped the poor, the Rosarians helped condemned felons during the last days before their execution; the "Sagrament" fraternities served during processions in honour of the Blessed Sacrament.

Regrettably, this picturesque reminder of the devotion of the Maltese is fast dying out.

90. St. Lucy – Valletta

S t. Lucy's is a "daughter" of the Collegiate church of St. Paul of Valletta.

It was built in 1570, only four years after the building of the city began. It was originally dedicated to St. Francis of Paola, a statue of whom is on the corner of St. Lucy Street, just opposite the church. The first Dominicans who went to Valletta from Birgu after the Great Siege administered the Sacraments from this little chuch, from which they moved to their new church of Our Lady of Porto Salvo in 1571.

The church was rebuilt with money paid by the wine merchants of the port who used to pay also for the expenses of the festa. It was then dedicated to St. Lucy and St. Vincent Ferrer.

The Third Order of the "minimi" of St. Francis of Paola was instituted in this church by Bishop Alpheran de Bussan in 1740.

The titular painting is of Our Lady, Mary Immaculate, with St. Paul, St. Lucy, St. Vincent Ferrer, and St. Clare. The front of the main altar is decorated with baroque sculpture. Under this altar lies the body of St. Lucidian, martyr.

The side altars are dedicated to St. Francis of Paola and St. Pascal Baylon. There are statues of St. Lucy, St. Joseph, St. Francis of Paola, an Ecce Homo, and a statuette of Our Lady.

The bell-tower is right atop the façade and has three bells. It is surmounted by a statue of St. Paul, and has two niches with statues of St. Clare and St. Lucy.

The pavement is in marble, and also in marble are two of the altars. There are two silver lamps.

Mass is celebrated on Saturdays.

THE MARIAN CHURCHES

The Virgin Mary is widely venerated in these islands. As in Spain and Italy various titles are given to the shrines and churches dedicated to her. Thus, besides the universal Assumption, Nativity, Sorrows, Immaculate Conception, Carmel, there are curious names such as: of the ruins, of happy delivery, of the snows, ransom, mercy, patronage, perpetual succour, the forgotten, of the grotto, the dusky one, of providence, hope, virtue, graces, light, good counsel, of the souls in Purgatory, of the rocks, of the holy Rosary.

Curious names, but indicative of the affection and the trust our fathers reposed in the universal Mother.

91. Our Lady "Tal-Ħerba" – Birkirkara

According to Bishop Molina this was one of the oldest churches dedicated to Our Lady. It is also one of the most venerated.

The name, tal-Ħerba, "of the ruins" seems to indicate the state of the site when the church was built. Devotion to this sanctuary flared up when once a paralytic was suddenly cured and, dropping his crutches, stood up erect and walked away. He then roamed all over the islands proclaiming the miraculous healing. People flocked to the church and penitential pilgrimages were organised, especially in times of drought, famine or the plague. The church possesses very many votive offerings, including hundreds of "ex votos", crutches, iron shoes, chains left by liberated slaves, ropes and cables offered by sailors saved from drowning, many mementoes in gold, silver and precious stones offered in thanksgiving for healing obtained through the intercession of the Madonna. These mementoes took the form of images of part of the body, such as pairs of eyes, arms and legs.

Although the titular painting is of Our Lady of Graces, Bishop Cagliares (1615) wrote that the church was dedicated to the Assumption. The church was rebuilt in 1640 with funds contributed by the faithful. A single bell then hung from a tripod. Bishop Bueno (1668) wrote that the church was named after the Birth of Our Lady, but that the side chapel was Tal-Ħerba. And Bishop Alpheran (1736) recounts that the feast was held on the 8th September.

The old titular painting, now kept in the side chapel, shows Our Lady, flanked by St. Joseph and St. John the Baptist, showering graces on the souls in Purgatory. At the bottom of the picture there is the knight De St. Pierre who paid for the painting, and his coat of arms. The titular painting in the choir is a copy of the old one, but shows the Guardian Angel instead of St. Joseph. This was done in 1668-79. The side chapel, built in 1774 and decorated with sculpture has two statues representing Faith and Charity. Next to this side chapel is the belfry with five bells, the largest of which was made by Anton Tanti and blessed in 1713. In the year 1775 the relics of the martyr Saint Victoria were brought from Rome. They were kept in the church until the Dean, Canon Karm Sammut caused them to be incorporated in a statue of the saint.

The main altar enjoys a perpetual privilege granted by Pope Pius IV on 31st. July, 1776 and confirmed by Pope Pius IX on 28th June, 1857. Bishop Labini consecrated the church on 23rd March, 1783. This is commemorated on the second Sunday after Easter. Bishop Pace Forno instituted the congregation of Christian Doctrine in 1857.

With the approval of the Vatican the image of Our Lady tal-Ħerba was crowned by Bishop Pietru Pace assisted by Mgr. G. M. Camilleri, Bishop of Gozo, and the Cathedral Chapter. Witnesses were the judges A. Micallef and A. Parnis and among those who took part in the ceremony were the religious communities and the Camera Pontificia. Giuseppe Borg and the ex-procurator of the sanctuary, Constantine Grech, paid for the crown. The diamonds were taken from the votive offerings. Dun Alphonse Borg paid for the crown of the Child Jesus. The coronation took place in the Parish Church, the painting being then carried in procession to Tal-Ħerba. The event was solemnly commemorated in August 1960. Also in commemoration of the crowning, since 1967, the festa began to be held in August instead of in September.

The enlargement of the church started on 8th March, 1923, under the supervision of Architect Edwin Vassallo. Ernesto Pace donated the site. The church now is in the form of a latin cross, the old one forming the nave. The oratory, sacristy, belfry, and the side chapel were not altered. The new church possesses an elegant dome. Just inside the door, on the marble pavement, is an inscription: "when you enter this temple remember that the Lord blessed it and Mary chose it for herself."

A statue of St. Expeditus stands on the right, and that of St. Victoria on the left. Other statues are of St. Joseph, St. Aloysius, and of the Sacred Heart of Jesus. The relics of the Saints Vincent, Innocent, Urbanus and Faustus are venerated in this church.

As was to be expected the Knights of St. John of Jerusalem showed their veneration to the sanctuary with precious gifts. Besides the painting by De St. Pierre there is a small silver bell and a paten, bearing the coat-of-arms of a knight; a baroque altar frontal in silver on red velvet, given by Chev. Romualdo Doz in 1700; a silver chalice and aspersorium, both bearing the coat of arms of Grandmaster De Rohan. A small silver lamp covered with "fleurs de lis" could be a gift from Grand Master Wignacourt. Perhaps the most curious of the gifts is a bouquet of flowers made of seashells and tinsel having at its centre the figure of a woman bearing a flag and treading on a Turk. This could be a gift of La Vallette after the victory of the Great Siege.

Besides the gifts made by the knights there are two silver sanctuary lamps given by an unknown donor in 1786, six large silver candlesticks, censer, monstrance, incense-boat, and two silver reliquaries (1756), an aspersorium (1789) and a set of silver "gloria" frames, given by a certain Barbara (1776).

Of recent date is the painting on the ceiling by Prof. G. Briffa showing episodes from the life of Our

Lady, Old Testment figures and the Popes who honoured the sanctuary. Silver altar statues of the Evangelists and a blue velvet curtain are later additions.

Mass is said daily. On Wednesdays and Saturdays many people visit the sanctuary, which is very well kept, and religious movements hold their meetings in it.

92. Our Lady tal-Ħlas – Qormi

This is one of the most highly venerated Marian sanctuaries. Being situated half-way between Birgu and Mdina, it was in the past a convenient resting-place for those travelling between these towns at a time when they were the most important on the island. The original church, now a sacristy, was built around the year 1500, close to a cemetery. In the year 1560 the Treasurer of the Order of St. John, Fra. Christophe le Boulleur de Montgauldry, who had a house by the church, built a room for the rector in the garden close by. His coat of arms appears on its wall. Montgauldry was a great benefactor of the church, building it anew and paying for the titular painting, now kept in the sacristy, which showed Our Lady with St. Paul and St. John the Baptist and bore the arms of Montgauldry and the date 1573.

The Bishops, in the reports of their pastoral visits, as well as Mgr. Dusina, mentioned the veneration in which the church was held and the large number of *ex votos* kept in it. From one of the reports we know that the church was enlarged in 1634.

Tal-Ħlas was seriously damaged in the violent earthquake of 11th January, 1693. It had to be rebuilt, the architect being Lorenzo Gafà. The titular painting of Our Lady Tal-Ħlas (protectress of mothers in labour) was placed above the old one.

Pope Clement XI confirmed that the church fell within the parochial limits of Qormi. This is commemorated by his coat of arms on the façade of the church. The organ came from the Cathedral which, like Tal-Ħlas, had suffered grieviously in the earthquake.

Tal-Ħlas possesses several paintings, including the coronation of Our Lady by the Blessed Trinity, done by H. Arnaux in 1719, as reported by Bishop Gori Mancini. The new titular painting is by Francesco Żahra. Other paintings show St. Thomas, St. Isidore, St. Pancras and Our Lady of Sorrows, the latter by Toni Falzon. The silver chalice was made in 1758 during the rectorship of Dun Alwiġ de Celis. The statue of the Assumption, in front of the church, is by Vincent de Candia, and was made in 1867.

The church enjoys bequests for the celebration of a sung Mass on the 15th August, and other Masses for which Wistin Vial left 75 scudi. (*Acts of Notary Gian Battista Curvisieri*). Another foundation for Masses was made by Dun Ġwann Ċilia, from rent on a house at 218/9 Main Street Qormi. (*Acts of Notary Ġużeppi Pace of 20th July, 1915*).

The loggia at the side of the main door, with stone benches and tables, was built in 1699 to afford a shelter for the numerous pilgrims who visited the church. It was rebuilt after the last war during which the church was used by the military. Pilgrimages to this sanctuary are still frequent. Many mothers present their babies to Our Lady.

The feast, which used to be held on the 15th August, is now celebrated on the Sunday following that date. In the past there was the custom of distributing hazelnuts and a glass of wine to visitors on the feast-day.

The church can be visited in the afternoons of Sundays and the principal feasts.

93. Our Lady "Tal-Patroċinju"
– Għasri, Gozo

This church is hidden down the deep Wied-il-Għasri valley. One can barely catch a glimpse of it from the Ta' Pinu-Għasri road. It is hidden from view even when one starts from Għasri on the road leading to it. The first thing one sees is a stone column bearing the village cross. Then, suddenly, at a road turning, it is there. It has one bell-tower and a lanternless cupola. A stone coat of arms above the door was disfigured either by the French of Napoleon, as many others were all over the islands by the apostles of "égalité", or during the early British period.

The church has three altars, the main one dedicated to the Madonna, the lateral ones respectively to St. Paul and St. Joseph. The beautiful painting of the main altar is probably by Żahra. There are other paintings, the coat of arms, on wood, of Pope Clement XIII, and two silver lamps made in 1740 and 1782. The first of these was donated by Fra Angelo Bonnici and hangs in front of the main altar. The other is in front of St. Joseph. Another lamp which used to hang in front of St. Paul was lost some years ago. From the cupola hangs an old crystal chandelier. The "palm" silk damask dates from 1851. A fine statue of Our Lady of Fatima is the gift of the Żammit family of Valletta.

Of interest is the main altar which is made of gozitan alabaster, honey-coloured, with red and gold flashes. This alabaster was found in 1738 in a field at iż-Żebbuġ.

An older church on the same site was built early in the sixteenth century. The present one was built in 1739 by Dun Tumas Saliba, a sacristy paid for by Dr. Fra Angelo Bonnici being added four years later. The priests of iż-Żebbuġ bought the sacred vestments.

The church was at first a subsidiary of the parish church of Żebbuġ, but at the instance of Dun Tumas and Fra Angelo it was placed directly under the Roman Lateran Basilica of St. John. It was consecrated by Bishop Vincenzo Labini on 10th May, 1789.

The village of Għasri was declared a parish in 1922. The Tal-Patroċinju church falls within its limits.

The festa is celebrated on the second Sunday in November. Mass is said every Sunday, on the first Saturday of each month, on the "Wednesdays of Santa Marija", on the days of the apparitions at Fatima, and on the 2nd Sunday after Pentecost, feast of the consecration of the church.

Until some years ago, on the day of the feast of the Espousal of Our Lady, the 23rd January, the Rector used at Mass to bless a quantity of almonds which he distributed to the faithful.

The second Rector of the Church, Dun Ġużepp Schembri (1776 - 1821) was a saintly man. It is said in Għasri that once he exorcised a dumb possessed man. On another occasion, during a period of severe drought, he flogged himself while delivering a sermon. That same night it rained. Graces are said to have been obtained through his intercession. He is said to be buried in one of the graves under the church floor.

After Dun Ġużepp there were six other Rectors.

LEGENDS

Tradition, legend, fairy tale: where does one end and the other begin? At what point does belief merge into credulity?

Tradition passes down accounts of true happenings from father to son. But a word added here, or another left out there; a pinch of misplaced enthusiasm; a little wishful thinking; a trace of doubt; and tradition becomes legend.

So, in legends it is perhaps worth while to look for an element of truth. Maybe the legendary figure is the personification of a belief, a fear, a patriotic feeling. The maid of Mosta hiding in a cave may represent hundreds of fugitives; and Żgugina's trust in St. Dimitri, the simple almost childlike faith of many of our forefathers.

Whatever their nature, legends are certainly a picturesque facet of folklore.

94. St. Matthew, tal-Maqluba – Qrendi

S t. Matthew's is made up of two contiguous churches, the smaller of which can barely house a dozen persons.

This smaller church, which has a window giving on the valley, and which resembles a crypt, is very old, and believed by some to date from the thirteenth century. It does not figure in the "rollo" drawn up for Bishop De Mello in 1436. In 1575 Mgr. Dusina reported that it possessed all that was needed for the divine office, but had neither funds nor encumbrances. The widow of Ninu Żammit, who held the lease of two fields, was obliged to pay for the singing of vespers and the celebration of a Mass on the saint's feast day. Up to 1618 St. Matthew's fell within the limits of the parish of Żurrieq.

The building of the bigger church began in 1674 and was completed in 1682. By that time the parish of Qrendi had been formed by dismembering from the Żurrieq parish the hamlets of Ħal Lew and Ħal Manin. Parish Priest Dun Dumink Formosa blessed the new church on the 12th September, 1683. The titular painting, a fine example of the art of Mattia Preti, was done in 1688, at the time when Cocco Palmeri was Bishop, and was paid for by the knight Nicolò Communet. The old painting was transferred to the sacristy. The organ gallery was added in 1834.

The feast of the saint, held on the 21 st September, is a popular festa similar to that of Mnarja (29th June) when people spend the night at the Buskett gardens. In the past toys and small clay figurines of statues of saints, priests and members of the fraternities used to be sold close to the church. Today a fair is held, the two band clubs of Qrendi organising it in turn. On the feast day the church is decorated with damask hangings.

The church was hit by a bomb on the 12th April, 1942. It was repaired by architect S. Privitera who effected some structural changes, including the building of belfries at the two corners of the façade and the removal of the central belfry. The parish priest at the time was Dun Mattew Magro.

The Mattia Preti was stolen some years ago, but was recovered and kept at the Cathedral Museum until police proceedings were completed.

Close to the church is a deep and wide pit, looking like a very large stone quarry. It is in fact a fault. According to tradition the earth subsided during an earthquake and a violent storm on the 24th November, 1343. A legend would have it that a number of people living in sin were suddenly engulfed, only one pious woman who was at the time in the old church escaping with her life. The chapel itself was shorn in two. According to another version the survivors were a number of nuns.

95. St. Demetrius – Għarb, Gozo

This church is built on the edge of the cliff called Ras San Mitri (St. Demetrius' Cape) not far from the Ta' Ġurdan lighthouse. It can be approached by a country road from Għarb.

An older church was built by Dun Franġisk Depena early in the fifteenth century. Monsignor Miguel Balaguer Camarasa deconsecrated it on 24th May, 1657.

Dun Mario Vella, by will in the acts of Notary Gavino Bonavita, dated 29th April, 1736, caused it to be rebuilt leaving an annual legacy of five scudi for its maintenance.

On 11th April, 1809 the archpriest of Għarb, Dun Publius Refalo, representing Bishop Ferdinando Mattei, blessed the chapel.

At the start of the second world war, at the request of the procurator Dun Paul Formosa, Papas Schirò, parish priest of the Greek Catholic community, celebrated Mass at this chapel which bears the name of a Greek saint.

There is at San Dimitri a stone altar. The altar-piece, showing St. Demetrius on horseback with a praying old woman and a young man in chains, was restored in 1937 by the gozitan Wistin Camilleri. The mosaic pavement was laid in 1935, and the walls were coated with mosaic in 1950. Other paintings represent St. Paul, St. Aristarchus (one of his companions in Malta), the Assumption and the Holy Face. The church has a small sacristy and a pleasant "zuntier".

The festa in honour of St. Demetrius is celebrated on the Sunday following the 9th October, with a sung mass, vespers and sacramental benediction.

The church is well looked after by the women's section of the Legion of Mary. The Archpriest of Għarb is the rector of St. Demetrius.

An old legend, mentioned by the historian Agius de Soldanis and forming the subject of poems by Marì Meilak and Ġużè Delia, relates the liberation from slavery of a young man who lived nearby. An old woman called Natalizja Cauchi and nicknamed Żgugina had an only son named Matthew. One night Barbary corsairs swooped on the island, broke into

Żgugina's house, knocked her down and made away with her son. The unfortunate woman ran weeping to St. Demetrius' chapel and poured out her heart in passionate prayer.

"San Dimitri, bring me back my son, and I'll light your lamp with a measure of oil."

St. Demetrius heard her supplication. She saw him moving in the painting, whence he rode out and set off in pursuit of the Turkish ship. Soon he was back holding the boy in his arms. Then he reentered the picture frame. But the horse's hoof-mark remained imprinted in the rock.

· According to another legend an earthquake toppled into the sea the rock on which the old chapel was built, but the chapel itself did not break up, and sailors and fishermen often said they saw Żgugina's lamp still burning under water!

Another version of the latter part of the legend is that after the collapse of rock and chapel a ship dropped anchor close by. The anchor stuck and could not be recovered. Accordingly a sailor dived overboard to try and pry it loose. When he did not resurface, another sailor went in to look for him. After a while both sailors surfaced and described how on the sea floor they had seen the chapel with the lamp in front of the painting still alight.

"Full fathom five ..."

96. Our Lady "Taż-Żejt" – Għarb, Gozo

This church is dedicated to the visit Our Lady made to her kinswoman St. Elizabeth. It is known also as "the lower church", "Tal-Virtù, and "Taż-Żejt". The latter name, meaning "of the oil" originated from an old legend.

A pious but very poor old woman eked out a scanty living from weaving. She had a particular devotion to Our Lady and never failed to go and pray at her shrine. It saddened her that her extreme poverty did not permit her to buy oil for the lamp, and she prayed the Madonna to provide the little money needed for the purpose. One day in May she picked a bunch of wild flowers to offer to the Lady. Soon afterwards she fell sick. During her illness a lady of great beauty appeared to her and said: "go to the church and take with you a jar, for you are going to need it." Next morning, when she approached the churchyard she noticed that from a crack in the wall water was trickling. But it flowed rather sluggishly. Indeed, on drawing nearer she realised it was oil. She collected some in her jar and trembling with excitement went to show it to the priest. The news spread rapidly all over Gozo, and people flocked to take some of the oil. But greedy persons brought along large jars which they filled and proceeded to sell the oil. Then fire instead of oil shot out. After this water gushed out for a very long time. Then, when two families that lived nearby and used this water quarrelled among themselves, the source dried up for good. Up to some years ago people pointed to a stone basin in which the water collected, but this has now been buried under concrete.

The "oil" church was built on the ruins of an older one which had been condemned by Bishop Balaguer Camarasa on 24th May, 1657. This can be seen from an inscription on the main door dating from the time of Bishop Astiria. On the 17th June 1663 Mgr. Balaguer gave permission for the rebuilding, which started in 1675 and was completed in 1678. The people of the village contributed towards the expense.

On the 29th August, 1679, Bishop Molina raised Għarb to the status of Parish, and Taż-Żejt was the parish church until 1725, when the present parish church was built.

Dun Ġammarì Camilleri was installed as the first parish priest by Dun Alessandro Maglione, the Bishop's Vicar, on 15th September, 1679.

The devotion of the Gozitans to this sanctuary rivalled that enjoyed by the Conception church of Qala. (q.v.) In times of drought and epidemics many were the votive processions to Taż-Żejt.

Although very distant from the target areas, the church was hit by German bombs on the 25th March and the 29th July, 1942. A lot of damage was done to the cemetery adjoining the church, and bomb scars can still be seen on the trunks of palm trees growing there. This cemetery serves the villages of Għarb and San Lawrenz. Frenċ Mercieca, a saintly man popularly known as Frenċ tal-Għarb is buried there, and his grave is visited by many devotees, both Gozitan and Maltese.

According to the report of the pastoral visit of Mons. Rull of 31st May 1760, the parish priest of Gharb used to go and bless the cemetery on the Sunday in the octave of All Souls, sing the "libera" and impart absolution. Bishop Rull ordered that the clergy and the fraternities of the parish should accompany the parish priest. This is still done on the 2nd November, when, after a function at the collegiate church the canons and the clergy walk in procession down to Taż-Żejt, sing vespers and lauds for the souls of the dead, celebrate a solemn Mass and bless the graves.

Pope Gregory XVI by decree dated 29th July, 1842, (exactly one hundred years prior to the German attack) granted a plenary indulgence to all who visited the sanctuary between the first vespers and sunset on the feast days of Our Lady, that is, the Assumption, the Immaculate Conception, the Purification, the Birth, Annunciation, Presentation (21st November) and Visitation.

The small parvis, the elegant bell-tower, topped by a statue of St. Paul, and particularly the cemetery, full of trees and plants, make this a really lovely church. It possesses three altars, all with metal candlesticks provided by the procurator, the Chevalier Paul Formosa in 1959, and a mosaic floor. The titular painting shows the Madonna and St. Joseph being received by Elizabeth and Zachary. It was painted in 1651. Victoria Micallef paid for it. It was restored in 1874 by Giovanni Gallucci who painted the dome of the Cathedral at Mdina. It is said that this painting was twice removed to the collegiate church, and twice was found back in its place at Taż-Żejt.

On either side of the main altar are good paintings, showing the Visitation and the election of Our Lady by the Holy Trinity to be the mother of the Saviour. They were done in 1967 by Paul Camilleri Cauchi.

The paintings at the other altars are of St. Francis of Assisi and of St. Mary Magdalen. The latter was probably the titular of a church which existed at Dwejra. Another painting of St. Anne, St. Joachim and Our Lady, was probably the titular of another chapel which existed in the Għarb district, near Wied il-Mielaħ.

Another important painting is that of the Assumption which is said to be the original one at

Ta' Pinu chapel, which had been deconsecrated by the Apostolic Visitor Mgr. Dusina, in 1575. A certain Mattew De Emmanuel, who was the procurator of Ta' Pinu had neglected the legacy left by a family for the celebration of Masses and necessary repairs. Dusina closed the chapel in accordance with the decrees of the Council of Trent, and ordered that the Masses be celebrated at the church of Għarb. Thus the old painting of Ta' Pinu remained at Taż-Żejt.

A precious painted leather altar-front was made in 1736. Wistin Camilleri made a fine crucifix in 1920 to replace one now kept at the Seminary. Another fine work by the Camilleri family, this time by Alfred, a Via Crucis, composed of little statuary groups, was completed in 1966. Dun Alwiġ Mizzi, S.D.B., a benefactor of this church, paid Lm100 for it. The first Via Crucis had been made by Dun Ġużepp Żammit in 1879. Another gift of Dun Alwiġ is a statue of St. Joseph. There are also the stations of the Via Matris. The bigger of the two bells was installed in July 1902 at the instance of Archpriest Dun Frangisk Saverju Debrincat.

The stone baptismal font had been lent to the new parish churches of Ghasri and Munxar until they had one made for themselves. There are also a pyx and a chalice, both of silver.

In the acts of notary Isidoro Xuereb, dated 17th January, 1857, Ġużepp Cremona left a perpetual legacy of five scudi a year for the celebration of a sung Mass and a sermon at the altar of St. Francis on the feast of Our Lady of Sorrows. This is now celebrated at the parish church. Mass is said at Taż-Żejt on Sundays and feast days. The Legion of

Mary hold their meetings there. The feast is celebrated on the 3rd Sunday before the 31 st of May, the liturgical feast of the Visitation.

97. The Assumption "Taż-Żellieqa" – Għargħur

According to tradition, in the year 1560, Our Lady appeared to a maiden at this spot and cured her of a disease. The grateful young woman built the Żellieqa church. This is stated in Mgr. Dusina's report of 1575. Dusina wrote that the girl was still alive. His statement is repeated by the historian Abela Ciantar in his "Malta Illustrata", but no mention is made anywhere of the girl's name or the precise date of the apparition.

The church, always according to Abela Ciantar, was held in great veneration by the Maltese around the year 1760, at the time he was writing.

Achille Ferres states that the church, built in 1560, was rebuilt in 1650, the architect being the gifted Tommaso Dingli.

Of interest is the marble altar decorated with baroque sculpture. The painting of the Assumption is by Rocco Buhagiar. Two old paintings were originally in the Għargħur parish church. In 1962, Chev. Emvin Cremona executed a painting of the Virgin and the unknown maiden.

Two marble plaques, with Dusina's statement, in Latin and in Maltese, were uncovered in 1950. Mass is said on all Sundays and on the first Friday of each month. No collections are ever made but the faithful contribute generously.

The festa is held on the 15th August, when the church is decorated with damask hangings and the front is lit up. The Rosary is recited during the two weeks preceding the festa, at the end of which period a pilgrimage proceeds from the parish church. A solemn Mass with panegyric is celebrated on the feast day.

During the night of the 11th February, 1989, sacrilegious thieves stole a pyx, scattering consecrated Hosts in the process.

98. St. Martha – Victoria, Gozo

Halfway up the road from Mġarr which climbs to the Conservatory there is the small church of St. Martha, called "tal-għonq". Across the road from it is a cemetery where the victims of the cholera epidemic of 1865 are buried.

The church was built in 1866 in fulfilment of a vow made during the epidemic. The Vicar General, Mons. Pietro Pace, laid the first stone. Building was completed on 11th November, 1866.

The painting on the main altar, the work of Pawlu

Cuschieri, was done a year later. The two bells, cast
in 1864 and 1867 respectively are the work of Salvu
Cauchi and his brothers.

In 1938 a mosaic pavement was laid. A fine statue
of Our Lady of Graces, which had stood in front of
St. Martha's since 1866 was in 1893 moved to the
Conservatory grounds where it can still be seen. A
statue of St. Martha, by Albert Micallef, was blessed
by the Bishop of Gozo on 27th July, 1988.

The feast is celebrated on the 29th July. For a long
time Mass was said daily at mid-day. The practice
has been discontinued, but Mass is celebrated on the
day of the festa, every first Monday of each month,
and during the whole month of November, daily, at
6 p.m. On the 1st November the Rabat clergy sing
the lauds from the Office of the Dead. The Rector
then blesses the cemetery and the "libera" is sung.
Although by no means an ancient church, Tal-Għonq
has its legends. It was said that the sexton once heard
the bell ring for Mass. Glancing at the clock he saw
it was already 5 a.m., so he hurried to the church
where he found an unknown priest preparing to say
Mass. At the termination of the sacrifice the priest
vanished. Back home, the mystified and shaken
sexton again looked at the clock. It showed 2 a.m.
Nobody seems to know exactly when this happened,
or even who the sexton was. But the story is similar
to the one told about Tal-Virtù church of Rabat. (q.v.)

Another popular story is that Toni Caruana, a
Rabat cobbler, used to collect contributions for
Masses for the repose of the souls of those buried at
Tal-Għonq cemetery, where he used to keep the
lamps alight during the month of November. He said

that on more than one occasion he had seen the dead moving in procession, and claimed that he recognised some of them!

Yet another similarity with Tal-Virtù church was the practice of throwing pennies through the church-door grille for the purchase of oil.

99. Our Lady of Mercy
– Xewkija, Gozo

This small church stands at the spot where the Xewkija-Qala and the Victoria-Mgarr roads cross.

According to Achille Ferres, as long ago as the year 1397 there was on this spot a church dedicated to St. Bartholomew. It must have been neglected and collapsed because there is no mention of it in Mgr. Dusina's report (1575). Yet, the historian Agius De Soldanis states that he had read in old documents that it was still standing in 1597.

It was rebuilt in 1643 by Notary Gian Paolo de Lorenzo on land coming to him from the dowry of his wife, Petronilla Pontremoli, following the issuing of a decree by Bishop Balaguer Camarasa dated 5th June, 1642. Petronilla had pledged herself to keep alight the altar lamp, to pay the expenses of the festa, and to provide all that was necessary for the upkeep of the church. This notwithstanding, the same Bishop after only fifteen years deconsecrated the chapel. But in 1674 Petronilla pressed for its reopening offering to endow it with the revenue from some land at Tar-Ramla which she had inherited from Canon Salvu Pontremoli. Bishop Astiria gave his approval when Petronilla promised to celebrate the feast and to distribute bread to all the poor who visited the church on that day.

Around the year 1709 Felić Axiaq built a loggia on the graveyard.

In 1735, when Dun Piet Aquilina was parish priest of Xewkija, the painting of St. Bartholomew was replaced by one showing Our Lady with St. Bartholomew and the souls in Purgatory, the work of Gian Nikola Buhagiar. A certain Orazju Gilestri paid for it. Since then the church has been known by the name of Our Lady of Mercy. In 1870 the painting was restored by Busuttil.

In the year 1798, when the island of Gozo rose against the French, a fierce fight took place around a well there was on the zuntier. All the frenchmen were killed. One of them, who was found to be wearing the scapular of Our Lady was buried in the zuntier. All the others were dumped into the well which continued to be called "the well of the frenchmen."

Between the years 1846 and 1856 a pious hermit named Fra Bernard used to live in a room above the sacristy. An interesting story is told about him. He possessed a golden chalice. A thief who wished to steal it knocked on his door one night while a fierce storm was raging. He asked him to go and assist his father who was dying. This was a lie, as his father was in excellent health. The hermit replied that it was useless to go because his father was already dead. In fact he had been struck by a thunderbolt. The thief repented, became a hermit like Fra Bernard and lived a saintly life.

At the end of the nineteenth century the Pontremoli family lost interest in the church, and in 1895 it was taken over by Parish Priest P.P. Ciantar, who effected some repairs.

In 1933, under Dun Ġużepp Attard the church was given a new lease of life, for it was enlarged, improvements were made in it, and it began to be used more intensively in the pastoral work of the parish. Dun Ġużepp built a new sacristy and a large hall for the teaching of the catechism. At the same time the Xerri brothers gave some land to be used for widening the yard.

On the 13th December, 1944 the Dominican nuns took over the management of the church. In 1955 they widened it and on the 10th February, 1967, Bishop Pace blessed the church and the school opened by the nuns.

The nuns are rendering sterling service. Besides conducting a kindergarten they organise meetings for the Legion of Mary.

Mass is celebrated daily, and the Rosary is recited.

Every Thursday there is an hour's adoration of the Blessed Sacrament. Every two months the adoration lasts the whole night. Catechism is taught and the feasts in honour of Our Lady (17th September) and St. Bartholomew (24th August) are celebrated.

100. Our Lady of Carmel
– Fawwara, Siġġiewi

The church is reached by following the road from Siġġiewi to Rabat until one comes upon a statue of a soul in Purgatory, then turning left and carrying on beyond the Church of the Annunciation of Fawwara.

The spring which gives the place its name rises in a tunnel below the church. The field in front of this tunnel used to be a large water cistern.

The story goes that once, at a time of great drought when the spring had dried up, Ġerolama

Ciantar, who owned the fields in the vicinity, made a vow to build a church if the water started to flow again. Water did flow, copiously, and Ġerolama fulfilled the vow. The foundation was made in the acts of Notary Pietro Paolo Vincella on the 5th March, 1616. Ciantar bequeathed her fields to the Brotherhood of Our Lady of Charity of St. Paul's in Valletta. A plaque on the side of the church, dated 1616 commemorates this donation. According to the same plaque the church was rebuilt in the year 1669 by the Venerable Brotherhood at the time when Pasquale Bonanno was procurator.

Always on the same plaque there appears the name of another procurator, Antonio Palma, and the year 1756. Presumably that year the church was again restored.

The Brotherhood took good care of the church. Towards the end of the past century Government took possession of the water of the spring to supply all the Cottonera district. In exchange for the spring and the adjacent land the Government ceded other lands to the church. With these revenues the church could be furnished with everything required for the divine service and for various religious activities.

The feast is celebrated on the Sunday following the feast of Our Lady of Carmel of Valletta. The Brotherhood, which has around sixty members, celebrate the occasion by repairing to Fawwara for what must be a very enjoyable day of relaxation in ideal surroundings, the view from the terrace providing one of the most picturesque views, with the sea and the rock of Filfla right opposite.

Above the door of the church is a stone coat of arms, unfortunately indecipherable, and under it the emblem of the Brotherhood, with the motto "Charitas". The strikingly beautiful titular painting, restored some years ago, shows Our Lady, and Child, both crowned and having at their feet St. Catherine of Alexandria and St. Jerome. At the bottom appear two hooded brothers with the emblem of the Brotherhood between them. Still lower is the Ciantar coat of arms, the letters G.C. and the year 1674. Above the painting is yet another large emblem of the Brotherhood.

Worthy of note is the Via Crucis made of round mother-of-pearl shells, each eight inches in diameter, mounted on wood. In the sacristy is a sculptured stone lavabo.

As the church is quite small there is no organ gallery. The harmonium is therefore ensconced in one of the deep windows high up the side walls.

Mass is celebrated every Sunday at 11 a.m.

Acknowledgement

The invaluable help of many friends in the preparation of this book is gratefully acknowledged. I feel particularly indebted to Mr. Mario Buhagiar, Dun Ġwann Azzopardi, Dun Nikol Vella Apap, Fr. Alexander Bonnici, O.F.M. Conv, Dr. Godfrey Wettinger, Mr. Maurice Busetta, and Messrs. Walter and Trevor Zahra.